Mrs Mills Solves All Your Problems

Wit and Wisdom from the
Sunday Times Agony Diva

Edited by D.J. Mills

MAINSTREAM
PUBLISHING

EDINBURGH AND LONDON

First published in Great Britain in 2007 by
MAINSTREAM PUBLISHING COMPANY
(EDINBURGH) LTD
7 Albany Street
Edinburgh EH1 3UG

ISBN 9781845962869

All illustrations © Gavin Reece

A catalogue record for this book is available
from the British Library

Typeset in Century Old Style and Century Gothic

Printed in Great Britain by
Clays Ltd, St Ives plc

CONTENTS

Who is Mrs Mills?

PERHAPS THERE WAS SOMETHING IN THE AIR. A new century was about to begin. People were looking for answers. *The Sunday Times* turned to a young, straight-talking mother of three.

None of us could have guessed back then that Mrs Mills' column would continue for so long or prove so popular. Indeed, initially none of us knew what she was going to write about from one week to the next. As it was driven by readers' letters, it could cover anything. Was it an etiquette column? Sometimes. Was it an agony column? Very often. Did it contain useful household tips and cleaning hints? Yes. Could it improve your sexual technique? Possibly.

Mrs Mills could handle anything the readers threw at her. Having known and dealt with her all this time, I am not surprised. Mrs Mills is formidably able. Of course, she knows, as you will realise, all the finer points of etiquette, but just as importantly she understands how irrelevant they can be. She believes in good manners, deploring boorishness above all. Her insight and analysis of the dilemmas of contemporary relationships are legendary. Her pronouncements on the moral conundrums of twenty-first-century life should be enshrined in law.

The first letter that Mrs Mills dealt with in the opening column set the tone:

My best friend has a novel coming out. It's terrible, and the reviewers will slay her. She's bound to ask my opinion in front of other people. How do I answer without offending her or making myself look a fool in front of others by saying it is good? (I can hardly say I haven't read it.)
Ms RL, Hampstead, London

Remember, society only remains civilised because people lie through their teeth. Spend the next two months wearing dark glasses. Thus, when the dread moment comes, you can say you have a rare eye complaint and have not been able to read anything.

Where does her expertise come from? She would modestly say it is just the application of the lessons of life, combined with a prodigious depth of reading, a classical education, the experience of child rearing, the lessons learnt on her grandmother's knee ('It was being so cheerful as kept us going'; 'Never throw away butter wrappers'; 'You can be under-dressed but never over-dressed'; 'Never trust a man in suede shoes'), a deeply suspicious mind and a sceptical approach to anything that involves a correspondence course, 'expert', guru, therapist, healer or the words 'holistic' or 'alternative'.

Why is she never seen? Mrs Mills deplores the feverish obsession with celebrity that has consumed modern society. She feels it would be demeaning were her photograph ever to appear in a magazine with an identifying caption. In fact, her face has appeared in numerous publications without their editors realising it, as she is an inveterate party-goer and often out at film premieres, theatrical first nights and gala evenings at the opera, but she moves unrecognised, and that's the way she prefers it.

This principled stand has occasionally drawn strong criticism from correspondents, and Mrs Mills has been moved to respond in print:

Dear Mrs S and Mrs J of Amersham, of course the letters are genuine and I exist, or do you think I am a monkey hitting the keys at random while lashed to a chair in the corner of the office between AA Gill's trouser press and Jeremy Clarkson's chaise longue? I am not publishing your letter, however, because it is too boring. Satisfied?

Numerous men entertain the most lurid fantasies about Mrs Mills and bombard her with letters, questionable drawings and hilarious photographs. On the other hand, there are some people, like Ms LB of Peterborough, who are convinced that she 'must be a man' and seek reassurance. Mrs Mills replied: 'Only last night Mr Mills reaffirmed my essential femininity. Several times.'

Of course, the great joy of Mrs Mills for most of us is that she doesn't sugar her words but delivers her advice straight. Some readers can find this upsetting. For instance, JM from Cork wrote to say:

> Judging by your answers to people's problems, you must be the most sarcastic, insensitive, stupid bitch around. Your answer to the poor woman who is worried about a hairy upper lip compelled me to write to you – you've driven me mad for a long time, but I was reluctant to upset you. However, seeing as you don't mind upsetting other people, I now don't care and hope this does hurt.

Mrs Mills wrote simply: 'I couldn't help but notice that your house is called Sloe Cottage.'

Of course, most readers admire Mrs Mills enormously, and she has a devoted following. Indeed, just a few months ago, Mrs RM emailed her to say: 'I so love your wit and wisdom and have been making a scrapbook of your problem column. It would be ever so helpful if you would compile your weekly advice into a book.' Well, Mrs RM, here it is.

How to Deal with Your Loved Ones

Relationships

PROCREATION, AS SHAGGING USED TO BE CALLED, is said to be the primal urge, the reason we are put on earth. Perhaps it is an urge so desperate that we can end up with a spotty accountant from Purley, or perhaps that's just ill-advised consumption of warm white wine at the office party.

We are not supposed to have hang-ups now. We are meant to be unrepressed, able to express ourselves freely and directly, liberated sexually and morally, and living in an age where the power balance has shifted and men are no longer in charge. Sadly, this does not seem to be the case. Women still put up with the most ridiculous behaviour from men. It never ceases to amaze me just how much women will tolerate. Close proximity seems to bring on moral blindness or deep stupidity. To many women, my response could nearly always be: 'Pack your bags and leave the slovenly psychopath immediately.'

Repression is a tricky one. On the one hand, there is a laudable English reserve that makes for politeness and good manners; on the other, there's crippling shyness that creates pent-up frustration and feelings of sexual inadequacy. There's a poignancy in those letters wanting advice about plucking up the courage to speak to a young lady 'I have worked alongside for several years'. But in contrast to these wallflowers I receive letters of such eye-watering sexual detail that I don't know whether to suggest yoga or call the police. One regular correspondent sends me explicit diagrams of his fantasies, which he and his girlfriend regularly enact: one can only admire the combination of imagination and stamina, as well as the exquisite draughtsmanship.

Over the years, I have concluded that relationships rely on being (fairly) honest with each other. The occasional little fib ('You look lovely'; 'She wasn't even at the conference') is vital, just as it is important to get big issues out in the open ('I'd prefer it if your mother didn't stay every weekend'; 'OK, I did, but it was a long time ago, and he was much smaller than you').

My other top tip would be don't let things drift. Too many relationships linger on in a slowly decaying half-life for years simply because they have become a habit that's hard to break – it's easier to carry on than to face sorting out the CDs and books, let alone the emotional turmoil. This is especially bad for women who suddenly find themselves back on the singles market in their late thirties, when trying to hide an air of increasing desperation becomes ever more difficult as male contemporaries shack up with younger women and the available older men are only available because they are smelly, useless sad sacks. Recognise when a relationship is doomed to failure and end it quickly.

When a relationship is working well, get married (see next chapter).

Last year I had a brief relationship with a good friend. He ended it for 'personal reasons' and I swiftly got over it (although the friendship foundered). Since then I've heard many times (from him and others) that he would like to restart the relationship, but I have always refused. However, last week I heard he was seeing someone else, and suddenly he's become very attractive. Should I go after him, or is this just a passing phase?
Miss LT, Carlisle

He hasn't really become very attractive: demand alone has increased his value. It is like two people bidding for a piece of tat at an auction: just because they have pushed the price into thousands doesn't turn it into a work of art. Would you still want him if the other girl dumped him? No, I thought not. Useful tip: romantic involvement with close friends or family pets always ends in tears. What, by the way, are 'personal reasons'? I cannot conceive of any other kind for such a decision, unless the government has ruled that it is a criminal offence to date anyone from Carlisle.

My partner of some 20 years is driving me mad with his habits, and I am thinking of leaving him. To name but a few, he regularly blows his nose into the washbasin. His avid newspaper reading in the morning leaves his hands black, and, as he seldom washes his hands, he leaves black marks everywhere, on the fridge, cupboards, doors, etc. His table manners are abominable – noisy eating, elbows constantly on the table and rushing away halfway through a meal to watch a cretinous programme on television, leaving me still at the table. He is noisy in company, interrupting my conversation as well as everyone else's. I have pointed out all the above to him, but he sneeringly says I am too fastidious. What else should I say?
BL, Brighton

Bye-bye.

Do you think young couples would benefit from a trial separation before getting married?
MT, Shrewsbury

I know of several couples who were separated for years before they met, and they still ended up getting divorced. A cooling-off period after the first flush of romance (or 'lustful infatuation', to give it its technical name) may be a good idea after they have actually met, but such separations often lead to the irretrievable breakdown of the relationship. The man will rediscover the unfettered joys of Saturday nights down the pub (known by women as 'inability to commit') while the woman may suffer a related anxiety, often expressed in the phrase, 'We just don't seem to be going anywhere.' Usually this is what the rest of us call 'getting involved with someone else'.

My fiancé proposed to me at the end of last year. We got engaged and marry next month. I knew he had a brother but did not get to meet him until a few weeks ago, as he has been working in America. The brother is gorgeous, much more fun than my fiancé, and he has a better job. I know that he has feelings towards me but is repressing them for the sake of his brother. I think I have picked the wrong one. I'm having sleepless nights. I'd feel terrible about letting my fiancé down, not to mention upsetting both our families. What can I do?
RG, London NW6

The whole of the rest of your life is in the balance here. Marriage is not by any to be enterprised unadvisedly, lightly, or wantonly. Elope with the brother.

I have just begun a relationship with a man, and everything appears to be going well. However, I would like to have some outside reassurance and thought consulting a mystic would be a good idea. Where can I find one?
Ms GFD, Eastbourne

Very sensible – as long as you remember the other important rules: never trust a man whose name begins with a vowel; never wear red before the second Sunday after Epiphany; and always put your left shoe on first (except when south of the equator). Reputable mystics can be found in tastefully decorated caravans on the outer fringes of fairgrounds. Some sceptics say they are a poor substitute for friends, but this underestimates the power of the dark side, as the great Obi-Wan Kenobi so wisely put it.

I am in my mid-twenties, well travelled and enjoying the challenges of my chosen career. Disturbingly, however, my thoughts have recently turned to weddings, as I'd like to marry my significant other (yet to be found) before dropping sprogs in my thirties. Will this illicit desire to do the right thing cause my peers to shun me? Am I abnormal, and should I aspire to be a single supermum? What is the protocol for a career girl these days?
Miss AE, Rainham

Marriage is not yet such a taboo that it deserves to be thought of as 'disturbing' or 'illicit' – words once used to refer to extramarital sex or certain African regimes. If you do get married, you are more likely to be the one who shuns your peers. You will suspect your single female friends of having designs on Mr Perfect (your husband). Your work colleagues without children will lack all understanding of what it is like to be a parent. Nobody is abnormal – it's the rest of the world that's wrong.

I am the owner of a fine cactus plant, the gift of a former boyfriend. Since we parted some two years ago, the cactus has flourished and is now a superb specimen that I cherish. It has grown apace and is exhibiting a startling resemblance to an intimate part of the male anatomy. My new boyfriend hates it and says it must go. I am very fond of the plant and am loath to see it condemned or consigned to the shed, where I am sure it will wilt. I have searched for a gardening book that covers the pruning of cacti but without success. Can you advise me on the procedure, or perhaps you have another solution to my prickly problem?
WB, Tiverton

There is an obvious Freudian agenda at work here: the clash of phallocentric male with symbolic plant. Your boyfriend's self-confidence will gradually shrivel as the cactus surges upward. Ask yourself which will prove the more reliable over the years and dump the other one.

A couple of years ago, I fell unfathomably deeply in love with a man and was blissfully happy until it ended for no reason (his decision). A short while later, he begged forgiveness, seeing the error of his ways. Cautious, and driven by a strong sense of pride, I resisted. After a short interlude, he announced he was seeing somebody else, although she was 'not really his type'. I didn't interfere. After a year, he traced me, rather cunningly through an employer, to let me know the girl was pregnant, and he thought it was his duty to let me know that he was going to propose. I wished him well and then bawled in secret. I now have a wedding invitation, and, after a short discussion with him, it is apparent that he does not love her, but me instead. Ooh, eek. My dilemma is this: if I go to the wedding, I shall feel rather like Andie MacDowell at Hugh Grant's in *Four Weddings and a Funeral*. I am sure I might do some serious damage when the vicar asks a certain question. Can you advise me on what to do? Should I become a nun?
HS, Domme, France

This man is a complete twerp: first telling you that he was seeing somebody else and then, a year later, with the flimsy excuse of some pompous nonsense about 'duty', tracking you down to announce she is pregnant and they are to marry. I can't decide whether he is stupid or cruel. Obviously he is (and always has been, hence the ridiculous 'announcements') unsure about this other woman but too timid to do anything about it himself. He is trying to get you to extricate him. So, if you do want to do some serious damage at the wedding, stand up and denounce him for the shabby little coward he is.

I am some 14 years older than my boyfriend. When we met, he was a strapping 24 year old with a reasonable head of hair. However, he is about to celebrate his 40th birthday and is now almost totally bald. Surely it is not appropriate for him to refer to himself as a 'young toy boy' any more?
VG, Warks

No, it's not. Dump him immediately and get a younger version.

Several years ago, I became friendly with a young man at work, and, although I have since changed my job, we remain close. I value him as a platonic friend, but, sadly, he appears to view our relationship from a different perspective. Neither of us is romantically linked to anyone else, and it would seem he views me as fair game for something more physical. This is not what I want, and I have tried to tell him so, but I am fond of him and would hate to hurt his feelings. Things come to a head each February, when I receive a large Valentine card, flowers and/or chocolates from my friend. I have never reciprocated, for fear of encouraging him. I did consider sending him a little something to arrive on the 14th so he could impress his housemates but was worried this would give him the wrong impression. What do you suggest I do in the future?
Miss HP, Preston

The worrying phrases in your letter are 'several years ago' and 'neither of us is romantically linked to anyone else'. Face the facts: you're a couple of sad sacks and in a few years' time, if things carry on this way, you will be desperate for him. You are reluctant to accept his suit because, deep down, you think you can find someone better. However, you have written to me because you are beginning to have your doubts and wonder whether you shouldn't grab him while he's still available. You could snap him up now but still keep your eyes open in case someone more appealing turns up. A bird in the hand is a start.

One of the ladies in the office where I work, who is about 35 and single, has, up to now, tended to conceal what I suspected was a more-than-ample bosom. Clearly, she has recently purchased some new bras that show her assets off to great effect, and obviously she is enjoying it all. How can I congratulate

her on this noble gesture? It certainly has made going to work doubly worthwhile.
LVT, Solihull

Reaching that certain age, your colleague has realised that her marketing strategy needed revising. If you are single, you should say: 'How about dinner on Saturday night?' If you are married, you should say: 'How about dinner on Saturday night? My wife doesn't understand me, and I'm thinking of leaving her.' Any other remark commenting solely on her appearance is demeaning and sexist.

Thirty years ago, my wife ran off with my best friend and left me with two bawling kids. She subsequently stole the entire contents of the house and left me with a tape, 'Softly as I leave you', and a note, 'I've got everything', on the mantelshelf. What can I do to commemorate the anniversary of this event?
BTE, West Yorkshire

You could set up an historical re-enactment society, like those groups who fight Civil War battles on bank holiday weekends, and get them to ransack your house while you are out at work. You might even qualify for a lottery grant. Alternatively, you could rent a video and have a quiet night in (although there are no lottery grants available for this activity at the moment, the Arts Council is looking into it 'as a way of democratising accessibility to interactive participatory role-playing within an arts paradigm').

I am a 35-year-old bachelor with a decent job, good social skills and a nice flat. All my friends assume that I would like to settle down with a nice girl. I, however, have no such desire and would much rather have 'adventures' with no commitment promised or requested. The general assumption does not help my love life, because the ladies who would suit me are afraid I might get too close and those who are looking for something more serious I do not wish to hurt. What

should I say to my friends, or how should I behave so that everyone understands my motives?
SNE, Geneva

Everything depends on sending out the right signals. You want to be seen as suave, debonair and sophisticated yet a bit of a rogue, a man's man but with an eye for the ladies. Brightly coloured silk shirts unbuttoned to the navel revealing a manly expanse of chest with a couple of medallions nestling in your luxuriant chest hairs should do the trick nicely.

Being a shy young woman by nature, I would dearly love to master the use of the fan as a means of communicating with the opposite sex, like the Spanish ladies around here. However, I gather this is quite a complicated exercise. Could my eyelashes be just as effective?
CJ, Malaga, Spain

No – they would need to be so large that you would be forever toppling over. I used to be quite shy in my younger days, but, happily, I found a cure; coincidentally, it was Spanish: sherry. Several large glasses, or 'schooners' as we called them in our sophisticated circle, and my bashfulness was soon conquered. Of course, I did numerous things I now bitterly regret and several I only admitted to after being supplied with photographic evidence, so, on balance, it is not a method I would recommend.

My wife and I enjoy reading through the lonely hearts ads, but we do argue over GSOH. What does it mean? My wife says 'Good State of Health', but I say it must be 'Good Sense of Humour'. Who is right? Please give us the benefit of your wealth of knowledge.
PF, Wimbledon

GSOH stands for Good Size of Hand. Occasionally it is followed by NNTB (Nose Not Too Big). Why this should be, I have no idea. Sometimes you see GSH, for Good

Shorthand, and WLTM means Weigh Less Than Mother (obviously). GCH is Gas Central Heating. A good state of health is indicated by AMOT (All My Own Teeth) or AMOL (All My Own Limbs). 'Attractive' means nothing more than recognisably human, '30-something' is 45 and 'Prof' means profitable. N/S stands for no snogging and N/T for no tongues. 'Educ'd' means went to school, while 'varied interests' means anyone's in with a chance. 'No ties' indicates a casual dresser.

I am 75 years of age, in good health, good figure, play tennis, walk everywhere and carry all my shopping. What can I do to prevent men buzzing around me?
HH, Desford

Borrow a young man of 25 or so (a nephew, say) and have him escort you about the place for a few days. Accompanied by him, emerge from behind bushes adjusting your clothes, use inappropriate language for your age (such as inserting the word 'like' several times into every sentence, as in, 'I was like totally like freaked by it,' when discussing *Songs of Praise*), and start wearing miniskirts. I guarantee you will be left alone. Those men will be scared witless.

I have yet to master the art of keeping the woman in my life happy. As you are clearly a fulfilled married lady yourself, can you offer me any useful tips?
GS, Birmingham

As Mr Mills and I have found, there is no substitute for practice, practice and practice. On your own, if necessary.

I am in a long-term gay relationship and am often invited to the weddings of my lover's old school friends, whom I have hardly met. How on earth should I explain myself if the bride's father asks how I know the groom?
FGH, London

How about: 'I'm involved in a homosexual liaison with his friend George. We have been living together, in the fullest sense, for several years now, but there's nothing to be alarmed about: neither of us is given to hanging around public lavatories making a nuisance of ourselves (at least not as far as I'm aware). Naturally enough, most of our friends regard us as a couple – I say "most" because that little minx Damien still likes to think George has got a thing for him, which is just not, not, not true – though I think you'll find we both drink pints and we both like football (isn't Ronaldo just to die for?). OK, I'll concede we both have a thing about interior design and Judy Garland, but, hey, so do some straight guys, right? No, they don't really, do they? Gosh, is that the time? I must dash: I want to catch the bouquet.'

Call me naive and inexperienced if you must, but what exactly are 'sweet nothings' and how does one go about whispering them into one's lover's ears? Am I missing out on something?
REC, Somerset

Sweet nothings began to fade out during the last war and became extinct by 1963. They have been replaced by the phrase: 'Fancy a shag?'

I am convinced that evolution has developed the human brain to ask one overriding question when people see members of the opposite sex: 'Would I sleep with him/her?' I believe men have three answers to this: 'Yes', 'No', 'Possibly'. What answers do women have?
Dr JW, London

As you would expect, being subtler, more complex creatures, women have myriad responses: 'Now, and don't whimper', 'This should get that tap fixed', 'Oh, go on then', 'If you must, at least it'll be quick', 'All right, if I can stay awake', 'OK, you did buy dinner', 'Certainly not, just because you bought dinner . . .', 'After the way you referred to my mother, forget it', and 'Ha, ha, ha'.

I am 35 years old and single. Recently, I've found myself reading the Encounters section of the Sunday papers and giving it serious thought. I also realised that I actually enjoyed the company of the two fridge repairmen I had to call out on an emergency last Sunday. Is this just a phase or should I take action?
EB, Battersea

You could advertise: 'Desperately seeking n/s fridge repairman with GSOH and own tool kit.' But you don't really need the lonely hearts ads, just work your way through the Yellow Pages.

Where did men pick their noses before cars were invented?
NE, Dublin

On horseback, in stagecoaches, walking down the street, lying in bed, standing in pubs, while talking on street corners, while watching cockfights or writing sonnets, sitting in Parliament, in fact any time they imagined their wives weren't watching (and sometimes even when their wives were if they had 'just got hold of a good one').

I have been dating a girl for several months now, and our relationship is full and very open. My problem is that I have to keep my socks on during sex, as I have only three toes on my left foot. My partner complains continually about the sock wearing, and I would remove them in an instant, but my previous girlfriend also complained, and when I did make love sockless she finished the relationship, aghast at the sight of my foot. My partner sees the sock wearing as a sign of disrespect, but I do not want to lose her. What can I do?
RDW, Manchester

Simply have another sock underneath the one you take off. Alternatively, invent some heart-rending story to explain the absence of two toes – the rescue of a kitten from the jaws of a ravening grizzly bear should do it – and she will love your feet more than the rest of you.

I have been a widow for 15 years and have been stepping out with a very nice gentleman friend who wants to marry me. When passing his house last week, I decided to pay a surprise visit, but the surprise was on me. I didn't ring the bell because the lounge curtains were drawn and I thought he might be having a nap after his lunch, but through a tiny gap I saw him doing yoga in the nude. It was not a pretty sight, and I was deeply shocked. Should I forget about this man on the grounds that he must be a pervert, or should I take up yoga myself?
DD, Bucks

You are obviously deeply ambivalent about this. It depends whether you liked what you saw, and you should consider yourself lucky to have had the opportunity to check out what you'll be getting before committing yourself to anything unpleasant. Practising yoga is not in itself perverted, although it does promote suppleness and so I suppose might be thought of as increasing the range of possibilities in the sexual gymnastics department. Then again, I suspect that at your age, keeping it simple would be best (please, no photographic evidence of your abilities to the contrary. I am still in shock from Mrs AB and the lederhosen. I never knew they came in such large sizes, though I admit that that zip looked really useful).

I would be most grateful if you could inform me of the correct etiquette regarding the ownership of photographs. I have recently finished a relationship with a girl, and she has refused to give up some photos she took of me in compromising situations. She said that I was a more than willing participant, it was her camera, her film, she took the photos and paid for the processing. Following our rather acrimonious split, she has threatened to send copies to my family, our mutual friends and my parishioners. What can I do to prevent this?
SJS, Suffolk

You could pay her a large sum of money for the negatives, but you shouldn't worry too much. In my experience, once people see these photographs you will become an object of admiration in your local community. Your feats will be celebrated, you will be greatly envied, and your congregation will swell a hundredfold. (The C of E is always wondering how to get them packing the aisles; you may have the answer.)

Do women with long tongues enjoy a better sex life?
JBP, Southampton

No, but their husbands and boyfriends do.

I have been dating someone who I like very much but who makes himself available to me only once a week, at most. When I suggested we increase the frequency of our trysts, he replied that he does not want to 'rush into things' or to have a relationship 'take over his life'. My friends assure me that his attitude is level headed and mature. My friend across the pond posits that it is 'self-centred' and 'controlling'. What do you think?
BJG, New York

Face the facts: he doesn't fancy you very much. So walk away from this failing relationship in a dignified manner. That'll show him who's in control (and tell as many people as you can of his physical inadequacies just to make yourself feel better).

I am having trouble persuading Isobel, my Spanish girlfriend, that when we marry in England she will take my initials and be known as Mrs CO Jones, rather than Senora I Jones. She says she would rather remain Senorita I Garcia. When I ask her why, she just laughs, makes what I take to be rude remarks in Spanish and says, 'What kind of a word is missus?' I don't want to lose her. Do you think I should change my name to hers?
COJ, Macclesfield

She is testing your machismo, as no Spanish girl wants to marry a wimp (most take Carmen as their role model). You need to assert your masculinity. Take up bullfighting. Generally, Spaniards can be very tricky. One minute they are smoulderingly gorgeous, the next, fat, frumpy and luxuriantly moustachioed.

Why is it as soon as I mention I am broke, women immediately pack their kit and beetle off like scalded cats? Paradoxically, up till this time they all swear they love me madly. Am I out of touch with reality?
NAA, Aberdeen

It amazes me that anyone could ever have thought men were the superior sex.

I have been enjoying a wonderfully uninhibited relationship with my girlfriend for the past three years. Now, my elderly, disabled mother has blackmailed me into allowing her to move in with me. Do you think this is likely to affect my relationship adversely?
NB, Berkhamsted

Without more information, I cannot give a definitive answer. If, for instance, you both like to watch *Antiques Roadshow* while going at it like knives, then I think your mother could be an inhibiting factor, but then again it may all come down to how good her hearing is.

On being invited to my boyfriend's parents for the first time, I eagerly took his advice to wear whatever I felt 'most comfortable in'. This happens to be a Bart Simpson T-shirt, white plimsolls with Teletubby socks, and fraying jeans worn with a big belt that has a smiling teddy-bear-face buckle. The parents' disappointment was palpable. Assuming I am invited back, am I expected to smarten up?
HSR, Basingstoke

What you wore sounds fine, but I don't think it is appropriate for a child of your age to have a boyfriend.

I find that I am unable to cope with my steamed-up spectacles when I'm in bed with my new girlfriend. She is very understanding and helpful in dealing with directional problems, but still I feel embarrassed that I need to be constantly dabbing at my glasses in a vain attempt to see what's going on. Do you have any advice for short-sighted people in this situation? (I am unable to wear contact lenses.)
AFG, London N6

As your only difficulty seems to be seeing what is going on rather than actually doing it, why don't you simply video the proceedings and you can watch later from the comfort of an armchair?

Every year, my mother knits me a woolly sweater of Bransonesque colouring. Sadly, my girlfriend gave me the ultimatum of her or the jumpers. I took them to a charity shop and thought that would be the end of the matter. However, last Sunday, while mowing my mother's lawn, I looked over the fence only to see the neighbour wearing last Christmas's sweater. What should I do?
AE, Glasgow

The most popular, charismatic men in Britain all wear dodgy jumpers – Richard Branson, Val Doonican and Gyles Brandreth – babe magnets all. Go back to the sweaters and get yourself a new girlfriend.

What can I do about my boyfriend? He seems to think he is a character from a Thomas Hardy novel. He dresses in period clothes and constantly checks the time on his fob watch. He cycles around on an old butcher's bike and is currently getting over the disappointment of not being able to have new lenses put in a pair of antique spectacles. Shall I give up my mobile phone and resort to using his wall-mounted dial telephone, or should I buy him a laptop and drag him into the twenty-first century?

FIW, Lincs

Join in with him in living in the last century in a Hardyesque way by refusing to have sex with him until you are married, yet all the while have a torrid affair with the local squire, as it is his right and your fate. Offer yourself for sale at the next village fete and suffer from a series of life-threatening illnesses – especially TB and pneumonia – refusing all medication except beef tea and leeches. He'll soon come to his senses (unless you expire first).

The latest lady in my son's life has confided to me that she has not yet 'consumed' their relationship. What am I to infer from this?

FAC, Oxfordshire

You had better buy a new outfit, ready for the wedding conception.

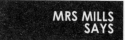

MRS MILLS SAYS   It amazes me that anyone could ever have thought men were the superior sex.

Married Life

GETTING MARRIED APPEARS TO BE SOMETHING of a minority sport these days, but I am a fan of it, though not in the way of those Hollywood stars who seem to like it so much that they do it repeatedly, clocking up a new wedding every couple of years. Once is enough.

People who 'live together' and call themselves 'partners' are just cowards hedging their bets, avoiding commitment and keeping their options open. Notice how a married man will say 'I'm married', where a cohabitee will invariably describe himself as 'single, but living with someone'. What he really means by this is 'living with someone until I fancy doing something/body else'.

Having found someone who is sane/hygienic/moderately interesting/almost solvent, snap them up and nail them down, I say. Just as a comedy is more than twice as funny when you watch it with someone and often rather depressing on your own, so life is much more fun with someone to laugh at it with.

It used to be that getting married was the only way most people could guarantee themselves any sort of sex life. This has ceased to be true, certainly since the 1960s. However, it has become increasingly clear to me that married couples are much more adventurous and experimental in the bedroom than the dreary unmarried. No doubt this is because a couple become more relaxed and confident with each other having put themselves within the bounds of a legal framework. Even if a suggestion is met with sniggering or shocked disgust, it is rarely fatal to the relationship, as long as the imaginative spouse knows when to back off and suggest tea instead. Research in recent years has shown that men, rather than women, seem to benefit disproportionately from being married, living significantly longer than bachelors. I like to believe that there's some connection with a healthily adventurous sex life rather than the fairly dull explanation that wives impose more sensible dietary regimes than most single men can be bothered with.

Of course, as the happy couple settle down into married life, new problems and challenges bubble up. The difficulties of sleeping together, now that it also means slumber as well as wild rutting, loom large in my correspondents' lives. Growing mutual incomprehension is a recurrent theme, too, but I like to think this can be enriching, as it shows that even those we think we are most familiar with still have the capacity to surprise us. Most couples seem to find a way to rub along together eventually, even if it means divorce.

I am about to get married and one thing nobody has yet mentioned is whether I should sleep on the left or right side of the bed. A married friend of mine, whom I asked recently, said that it all depended whether I was left- or right-handed. Don't you find this strange?
BA, Liverpool

The more incontinent partner should sleep nearer the door.

I have just discovered that my husband is having an affair with my brother. How should I react?
Mrs TR, Leatheringham

Oh dear, I bet you don't know which way to turn. Still, look on the bright side, at least you'll be able to rely on him to choose new curtains without you and there will be no more arguments when a Bette Davis film clashes with *Match of the Day*.

My wife refuses to be seen naked, even in the privacy of our own bedroom. How can our marriage be saved?
DC, Billericay

This is not necessarily a problem, unless the refusal to be seen naked also means a refusal to indulge in sexual activity. The naked human body, particularly past a certain age, is not especially exciting unless combined with a bit of sheer nylon, slithering silk, satin, chiffon or, every now and then, extremely tight black rubber. A woman should always preserve an air of mystery about her body. Indeed, my experience in various changing-rooms convinces me that many women would be well advised to wrap the mystery in an enigma and keep most of their clothes on and the lighting subdued. Of course, this is true of men, too. I have not seen Mr Mills naked for years, largely because whenever I did I was reduced to helpless giggles.

Many women want romance without sex, and many men want sex without romance. Could this be why so many marriages fail?
EG, Aberdeen

Not entirely. Sex, like romance, is an overrated part of marriage; a sensible washing-up rota is much more important.

Recent newspaper reports referred to a condition called 'recurrent coital amnesia' and explained that sufferers might call out strange names while making love or even forget what they were doing. Could you tell me more, as I think my husband may be afflicted with it?
HY, London NW8

I suspect it is more of an elaborate excuse than a medical breakthrough. So beware. The symptoms do not include sudden overnight business trips, unexplained items appearing on credit-card bills and a sudden tendency for men's aftershave to carry a hint of Rive Gauche.

Can you help me with a terrible problem? I am married to the most wonderful girl in the world, and although I work hard to keep her in the manner to which she has decided to become accustomed, I feel I have a right to a little nest egg that she knows nothing about. Unfortunately, she can smell money from a great distance, and cheques coming up the garden path are immediately sensed. I come home to find that letters addressed to me with money in them are already opened. I recently had to sign over some building-society shares to her for the same reason. How is a chap supposed to run a double life if his wife is watching him like a hawk all the time?
GP, Guildford

You need another address to which cheque payments can be sent and a bank account registered. A small flat is a good idea as it can also be used for clandestine assignations (sometimes called a 'long working lunch' or 'business trip') and even to house a mistress, although you may find that she opens all your post, too. However, your wife does sound wonderful: she has already got the measure of you and is keeping a beady eye on all your assets so that she gets her fair share when your divorce comes up.

For some time, my wife has been trying to buy a set of flying ducks for our home. Sadly, your publication recently revealed where these may be purchased. Do I (a) put my foot down and tell my wife she cannot order the offending items, (b) let her order the ducks but refuse to put them up on the wall, or (c) tell my wife to pack a suitcase and leave home as she has no taste?
BM, Liverpool

Compromise is always healthier. So put the ducks up on the wall then get up at dawn the next day. Wearing stout tweeds and waders, and armed with a shotgun, take up a crouching position behind the sofa and shoot them down. (I have, of course, lifted this answer from the forthcoming Labour policy document, 'Approved Alternatives to Hunting, Shooting, Fishing and Talking in a Loud, Confident, Patrician Manner'.)

My husband is one of the old school, preferring routine bedroom procedures, enlivened by the odd strangled snort, rather than anything more adventurous. I yearn to make love downstairs on the fireside rug to the strains of Brahms's *Requiem*. Must I endure years of boredom, or should I take the bull by the horns and insist on more adult entertainments?
DV, Norfolk

Many couples live in mutual isolation, separately imprisoned in private fantasies because they are too embarrassed to communicate their personal fetishes to each other. Knowing when to bring up the matter of chains, feathers or polystyrene is never easy, but it's best when the two of you are alone, rather than when you have friends over for dinner. Be prepared to compromise: initially, you may have to settle for taking the fireside rug up to the bedroom and having Radio 2 on. Be bold. It has always been my experience that as soon as you start confiding your fantasies you will discover your husband has secretly been harbouring just as many, too.

I always understood that women took husbands in order to have someone available to unscrew the tops off jars. After 18 years of marriage, my wife tells me there are other duties a husband is expected to perform. I disagree. Who is right?
BM, Dorchester

It is often said that society now is sexually obsessed. The television pours a torrent of filth into our homes every night (one needs at least two videos to keep on top of it), contraceptive devices are compulsory in schools, and magazines for men ('Blonde girl with no clothes on!') and women ('How to have orgasms!') can apparently write of little else. Yet, as both this and Mrs DV's letter show, there is a whole generation that seems oblivious of this revolution. You can always spot them: they are the ones who like knitting, gardening and polishing the car. Just remember that anyone with a hobby will have an inadequate sexual technique and you won't go far wrong.

A contemporary of mine has organised a reunion through our college publication to commemorate 40 years since graduation. It was an all-male institution then, and most of us have not seen each other during all this time, but the organiser has, out of courtesy I imagine, invited wives as well. My wife feels it is an occasion for men only, but when I made this known to a friend, who is also attending, his wife blew her top. 'You just want to be little children all over again, but I am going,' she blurted out. Is she being reasonable, and am I not lucky to have such an understanding wife?
KB, Aldershot

Of course you all want to relive your youth and, more importantly, boastfully exaggerate your achievements in the intervening years. The silly woman will be bored rigid. These women who want to storm the male bastions are woefully misguided. Don't they know how boring men are in large numbers? That men gather at such places as the MCC specifically to be boring. If a man starts relating an anecdote about the try he nearly scored for his old boys' team against Harlequins, any woman present will titter with incredulity, but other men listen respectfully, waiting for their cue to launch into some preposterous tale of a hat-trick against a Surrey second XI. Your friend's wife is a selfish spoilsport.

I am about to get married, and I have so far had conflicting views on whether I should buy a double bed or two singles. Could you throw some light on the matter?
WO, Gloucester

Certainly. It is quite clear you are not ready to get married (ask your doctor for a pamphlet). On the other hand, you might be marrying for money, in which case if your wife-to-be is particularly ugly I'd go for two singles, as you'll find waking up in the mornings slightly less distressing.

My wife likes to go away on craft weekends where she can improve her already considerable skills in pottery, pokerwork and macramé. While she is away, I take the chance to dress in her clothes and spend the evenings as my alter ego. Imagine my horror when, last week, just as I was putting the finishing touches in front of the mirror, I spotted the people opposite watching and gesticulating from their bedroom window. Now I dare not go out of the front door in case I meet them, and so hover around the back access. My wife is growing increasingly irritated by my odd behaviour and demands an explanation. How can I extricate myself from this situation?
ABN, Suffolk

You are going to have to confess, as your neighbours are bound to tell her at some point. You could say that you fell over in the bedroom and when you got up one of her dresses was stuck to you. Unfortunately, the people opposite misinterpreted your frantic attempts to pull it off. However, this will only work if you give up your cross-dressing fetish, and I fear this is unlikely, so why not bring it out into the open? Point out to your wife that she has a number of hobbies. You were feeling rather left behind so have been looking for a diverting pastime of your own. You have tried lepidoptery, practical car mechanics and building your own crystal set – dressing up in ladies' clothing seemed an obvious next step. Then go out to mow the front

lawn wearing a pink chiffon frock with your favourite briar clenched firmly in your manly jaw and give your peeping neighbour a cheery wave. If only people were prepared to be more open about transvestism, the world would be a much happier place (as the rest of us would be sniggering all the time).

My wife has recently purchased some new knickers. They are made of shiny nylon material, stretchy and very sexy. I have taken to wearing them, albeit without her knowledge. Our private life is deteriorating, but I wish to prolong it. Should I get into bed wearing her knickers, and if so what would her reaction be?
BW, Lincs

Why should I know what your wife's reaction would be? Mine would be to scream with laughter, and what an enemy of libido that is. Prancing about in ladies' undergarments is doing more for you than it would for your wife. On the whole, we women are not turned on by cross-dressing antics. We like romance and assured, yet sophisticated, masculinity. If you want to improve your 'private life', you need to start dressing and behaving like Cary Grant (that's Grant as he appeared in the films, rather than the real one who took LSD and crawled around on all fours yapping like a dog).

My husband is insisting we go to the supermarket with me wearing only a basque and stockings under my coat. He assures me other women do this. I'm afraid to ask my women friends for advice, so wondered if you and Mr Mills go shopping like that?
CS, Aberdeen

Agree to do it, but only if he reciprocates and wears an athletic support and the cardigan you knitted him for his bowls matches under his coat. Also, be careful when bending over the freezer cabinet in case he tries to take you by surprise. (Sainsbury's made such a fuss last month that Mr Mills and I haven't been back since.)

Newly married, my husband and I recently went on a pony-trekking holiday. Unfortunately, my mount was uncomfortably large, and it was all I could do to get my legs around it. My husband says I moan too much, but I feel I should write and complain as it's only this last week that I felt myself again. I asked him, but he merely simpered enigmatically and went back to his book. I did catch him consulting an encyclopedia the other week just minutes after I had told him the answer to his question (average rainfall in Uruguay, if memory serves). He mumbled something about 'just checking to make sure they had got it right'.
CP, Dunwich

Try it side-saddle next time. It may seem a little awkward at first (I always used to worry about slipping off), but you will soon get used to it.

My wife and I are both 28 and have been happily married for eight years. We have six lovely children but feel we never have any time to ourselves, and our marriage is starting to suffer. How can we find time to ourselves, bearing in mind our responsibility to our children? We feel life is passing us by.
S, Glasgow

Racking up six children in eight years sounds like more fun than most married couples manage, so spending time alone is perhaps the last thing you and your wife ought to do. Why not regard your children as a leisure resource? They could learn to play stringed instruments and explore the sextet repertoire of Brahms and Schoenberg. Otherwise, you will have to do what everybody else does and put your life on hold until the children are old enough to be ignored. It is your parental duty to be boring so that your children can rebel and thus feel they have an exciting life. Do not be seduced into thinking everyone else's is fun. (Most people assume, naturally enough, that Mr Mills and I lead a life of unparalleled glamour and sophistication, and, of course, we do, but we are rare exceptions.)

What can I do with my Spanish husband? I have two daughters aged one and two. The past couple of years have been hell, as my husband says he cannot sleep without the earplugs he has worn for the past 15 years. I am now expecting a third baby and dread another year of nights being up and down like a yo-yo with nobody to take over. He says that all I have to do is prod him and he'll get up, but when I've done that he demands to know why I've woken him up if I'm awake anyway.
JK, Madrid

Prod him in the back without yourself waking up. This is what I used to do to Mr Mills, and it was months before he twigged what I was up to. Unfortunately, when he did, he retaliated by prodding me back without waking up himself. This escalated until we were spending half an hour sparring with one another while still 'asleep'. We did find, however, that by then the baby had usually gone back to sleep anyway.

My wife has often told me that making love to me is rather less exciting than watching paint dry. As we near one of those red-letter anniversaries, I wondered if you had any helpful suggestions.
RT, Exeter

On the morning of your anniversary, paint the bedroom ceiling.

As a shy, retiring husband of many years' standing who has always been loath to initiate congress from fear of appearing bestial, I wonder if you could tell me if there is any way that a man can tell when his good lady wife is hot for it?
JD, Dublin

Heavens, after all this time if she is not ready now she never will be. It may be that your wife has given up and found some diverting hobby by way of sublimation: does she, for instance, show an inordinate interest

in the washing machine, endlessly relaundering the same load of sheets while fine-tuning the spin cycle? Any apparently pointless activity should be regarded as a cry for help.

I tried to get off washing up with a groin strain, but my wife says don't be silly, only footballers get strained groins. Has Mr Mills ever strained his groin? Was it a sports-related injury?
RK, Reading

He wouldn't dare.

My husband refuses to do anything about the hairs sprouting from his nostrils and ears on the grounds that 'it's nature's way'. What would you do in this situation?
MC, Rome

Give him raw meat and water for dinner.

My wife has an annoying habit of always leaving one object halfway up the staircase. I used to assume it was because it was to be taken up or brought down, but she can walk up and down a dozen times and it stays there. She also has an obsession with hanging things on the doorknobs (anything from bags full of used newspapers to pillowcases from the washing machine). Is there a cure?
DGNT, London W2

The most likely explanation is that your wife is a conceptual artist working with the dislocation of quotidian existence, turning the home itself into a site-specific artwork, following the example of Duchamp's inverted urinal. The everyday banality, for example, of a bag of washing is transmogrified by its provocative display from a door handle, just as the door handle itself is transfigured from its thoughtless state as functional object into the triumphant uselessness of

pure aesthetic experience. It is a work that proclaims: 'Behold, this is laundry!' and ineluctably carries within it all the associations of centuries of female oppression. Get your video camera out now and submit her efforts for next year's Turner prize. (Alternatively, your wife is a forgetful sloven with a lazy husband who does nothing to help around the house but is quite happy to moan about it.)

Why is it that when a wife discovers that her middle-aged husband is having an affair with a younger woman, he always says that it was a mistake, as if he'd inadvertently picked up the wrong trolley at the supermarket.
Mrs VN, Fleet

Let's face it, he does not always say it was a mistake. There's also 'I've never loved you' and 'You just don't understand me any more.' Of course, it all means the same thing – 'She goes like a rabbit and I'm terrified of getting old.'

My young son asked my wife why brides wore white. She answered that it's an old pagan custom to show purity and virginity. When he asked me the same question, I said it was because all domestic appliances come in white. Who is correct?
DS, Sheffield

Your wife: her reply is much funnier and more untruthful than yours.

My husband insists on wearing two types of gentleman's cologne. He splashes one brand on his face and neck, and another on his chest, armpits, etc. He says he does this so I will know where he is in the dark, but I feel that the overall effect can be quite unsubtle. Is there anything I can do?
CAC, Cheshire

Men can be cured of overindulging in cologne. It all depends on what upsets them. Some will give it up if you whisper, 'You smell lovely, just like Rupert Everett.' Others need a more interventionist approach. Secreting hair remover into the cologne that he slaps on his chest and armpits, for example, will terrify him into believing that he has developed some hideous allergy. Think what your husband's phobias are and work on them. Mr Mills had a passion for a particular obnoxious aftershave, but he poured it all away after I asked him why it was described as 'guaranteed to break the ice in public lavatories' in an article I claimed to have read in *Marie Claire*.

My husband is several years younger than myself but already affects the ways of a much older man. He lies in bed on his back with his mouth open, emitting fetid snores. When I jab him in the ribs to tell him about these unattractive ways, he responds with unnecessarily coarse language. What am I to do? I feel our relationship of many years is compromised.
Mrs BQ, Babbacombe

As they grow older, many men like to branch out and take up new hobbies, largely to compensate for failing powers in other areas of their lives. Sexual displacement activities is the term we Freudians use to describe golf, obsessive car cleaning and egg polishing (I haven't met a golfer yet who wasn't impotent). If your husband wants to pretend to be a much older man, I would thank heaven for small mercies.

In the 34th minute of the last cup final, the BBC commentator said, 'He put it in the right place but nowhere near hard enough.' My wife, who happened to be passing at the time, muttered something about this being the story of her life. I've been a worried man ever since. She's never once mentioned that she ever played football, and I'm wondering what other secrets

she's kept from me. Should I have it out with her, or forget the whole thing?
JC, Leicester

You ought to be overjoyed. Your wife has revealed that she is a knowledgeable football fan, so now you can share this passion.

My husband and I get sniggered at because I am a typical Amazonian woman in physique and height, while he is a modest 5 ft 8 in and only 9 st. What should my retort be to the sniggerers?
CB, Reading

'You should see the size of his wallet.'

When my husband finds himself sitting next to an attractive lady at dinner parties, he starts stroking her leg under the table. This is quite obvious to the other diners and embarrassing for me. Do I say something at the table and thereby draw attention to it or just ignore it?
Mrs MT, London W2

There is no need to say anything. At the top of your place setting, just next to the wine glass, you should find a glass of water. The next time your husband behaves in this way, pick up that glass and hurl the contents over him. Depending on how the lady concerned has been behaving you might also like to pick up the wine glass and deposit the contents of that over her, but I leave that to your judgement.

Since reading about James Bond in *The Sunday Times* recently, my husband has been intrigued by the idea of painting a woman gold. He wants to paint me, but in something more contemporary, perhaps Ronseal's Paint and Grain. Is this safe?
Mrs M, Co Meath

No, and the sanding-down to prepare the surface makes a right mess.

My hands and feet are usually cold, and this causes aggressive behaviour in the marital bed. I can get over the feet problem by wearing socks, but for some reason this sends my wife into hysterics. Can you recommend something to get my hands warm?
AB, Stafford

Place them between your wife's thighs. Not only will this take the chill off your hands it might also put the heat back in your marriage.

My wife likes to curl around me in bed. The problem is that I have very ticklish feet, and if she so much as brushes one of them with her toe, I start thrashing around in paroxysms. I have tried wearing bedsocks, but they were no help.
FF, Eastbourne

Wear shoes.

My wife sometimes goes to bed somewhat earlier than myself and is asleep when I arrive on the scene. The problem is that she sleeps diagonally across the bed, and, as a result, I have difficulty getting in. If I do manage it, I have to remain right on the edge of the bed. Should I erect a mini-partition to divide the bed into two separate areas, suggest that she spends more time with her mother or manhandle her into a non-trespassing position, even though this might precipitate her wrath?
BHDJ, Plymouth

Move the bed 45 degrees from its present position. Thus, when your wife gets into it she will be lying diagonally, but when you retire later, and she has been tossing and turning in her sleep, she will have moved herself into a straighter position and you can slip in beside her.

Alternatively, I find with Mr Mills that firmly planting a foot in the middle of his back and pushing hard usually means I can shove him into any position I like without waking him. (If I want to wake him, of course, I simply push that extra bit harder until he disappears over the edge of the bed. Colliding with the floor does the trick of rousing him from his gentle slumber, and we can continue the important and fascinating discussion about my insomnia.)

My wife wins all our arguments because she initiates them with the Hoover, blender or hair dryer in hand and switches the appliance on or off depending on who is speaking. How can I counteract this devious strategy?
EL, Gibraltar

Install a Tannoy system throughout the house, enabling you to broadcast your voice at sufficient volume to be heard above the drone of domestic appliances. Of course, the neighbours will hear you protest: 'Yes, I changed my underpants last week,' or whatever it is you happen to be arguing about, but you will probably think that a price worth paying.

I am considering putting my wife on a course of the new equivalent of Viagra for women. Have you ever tried it, and are there any contraindications? My wife is 49 years of age, and I am a hopeful 72.
JP, Southampton

I have not tried these pills and would not dream of doing so. It is the depressing cult of youth that insists an active sex life has to persist into old age. I am looking forward to serenity and calm wisdom, rising above the raging desires of my libido (as long as it happens after my 85th birthday, obviously).

Lights on or off? What do you think, Mrs Mills?
RAM, Manchester

What a bizarre question. On, of course, otherwise I tend to bump into things, and I find it much easier to read.

I am about to get married shortly to my childhood sweetheart. We are both very happy about the situation. We met at a party and hit it off great. We are both very much in love. There is one problem, however. My future wife objects to my choice of best man. I think he is an excellent choice. We've been friends since school. He is always neat and tidy. He speaks quite brilliantly on such occasions, or at least he did on the other four times I got married. How can I get her to change her mind about him?
R, Wolverhampton

You can easily persuade her by getting her to watch his previous speeches on video (you seem like just the sort of person to have had wedding videos made). I am sure that when she sees these, her mind will quickly be made up.

On several occasions now, I have returned from work to find that my wife has folded the end of the loo paper to give it a neat, sharp point. Do you think she has a hidden desire to run a guesthouse, or has she been having gentlemen callers during my absence? More importantly, should I refold the paper after taking a few sheets?
RI, Barkingside

You should do nothing of the sort. Your wife is going bonkers. Imitating the faux refinements of the worst sort of hotel in the home is absolutely terrifying. Where will it end? Imagine: little chocolates on your pillow last thing at night; tiny bottles of shampoo in the bathroom; lukewarm coffee, cold toast and an individual pat of runny butter for breakfast; a cursory knock on the door and a surly Colombian maid barging into the bedroom just as you and your wife are celebrating your anniversary in time-honoured fashion. And, when you attempt to leave the house, she will present you

with a bill for £835 that will include three phone calls to South America you never made, access to a dubious television channel and next door's newspaper bill. You must nip this one in the bud immediately: call in the local health and safety inspectors and get your house closed down because of the dangers it poses (bound to be the case: no private home would come up to the standards these people expect).

My husband used to be a marvel in the garden. He was always at it, whipping his hose out and bedding down, mulching and dibbling, or just forking away all afternoon. Now he says he's just not up to it any more. What can I do?
Mrs TRG, Whitstable

Try getting him interested in sex.

My wife of 35 years is having an affair, but my problem is not knowing how to break the news to her that I know and don't mind in the least. I could, of course, just come straight out with it and tell her, but she is a sensitive soul, believes I love her and would be devastated to know that I'm not bothered. Another course open to me is playing the part of the deceived husband, but I am a poor liar; she'd see through me in an instant. I could approach the man concerned, but I am sure he feels he has won my wife from me and I am loath to have him believe otherwise, for both their sakes. There is, by the way, no 'other woman'. What do you suggest?
HFL, East Sussex

There isn't really a problem here, is there? You just want to show off your sophistication.

My husband insists on feeding our cat at the table. From giving it an occasional morsel, he has progressed to sitting it on his knee to share his plate. Although I have pointed out that human food may not agree with a cat's stomach, he has now demanded that I

set a place for Tiddles (this is not the cat's real name), who, he claims, performs the role of food-taster. He read somewhere that Saddam Hussein refused to eat anything until it had been tasted first. I cannot help thinking that my husband is subconsciously criticising my cooking. How can I deal with this without appearing paranoid and so straining our marriage?
Mrs MTB, Lancs

Drown the cat.

My husband always shouts, 'Coming, ready or not!'
Mrs CS, Lewes

How very unsporting. You should refuse to play with him any more.

MRS MILLS SAYS

Sex, like romance, is an overrated part of marriage; a sensible washing-up rota is much more important.

Children

CHILDREN, ON THE WHOLE, ARE A GOOD THING and represent your best insurance for a comfortable old age. They can be a pain in the neck in the early years, but there is some compensation in their amusement value, especially their ability to be unabashedly rude in situations where you would like to be yourself but lack the guts to pronounce someone 'fat', 'smelly' or 'scary looking'.

Child rearing has changed dramatically over recent decades and not always for the better. I remember being mostly ignored by my parents, who seemed oblivious to my existence unless I was desperately ill or misbehaving outrageously. Consequently, for much of the time I was either undertaking something mildly dangerous (cooking slugs, wandering around the wrong side of town), or so screamingly bored I was driven to read a book.

Unstructured days are an anathema to today's parents who organise their offspring's lives in the minutest detail. A Sunday morning that does not include a hearty walk, a trip to a museum and a music lesson is a morning wasted. These parents then moan that they have no life of their own and that everything is done for the convenience of their children. Actually the reverse is true. Their children's lives are for their own convenience. The children would be quite happy mooching about on their own, but the adults force them into improving pastimes in order to bask in reflected glory. These are usually the children who are kept up late at night to see mummy when she comes home from work, but it is not the child who wants mummy, it's the mother wanting to assuage her guilt at being away from home and not having seen her baby all day.

Endless books are published these days explaining how to have babies and bring up children. Nervous parents snap them up. What's wrong with them? How do they think the human race managed to keep going in the millennia before this little publishing industry took off? I have quite a laissez-faire attitude to child rearing: as long as they are quiet and polite around me, I don't mind what they do. (Sadly, getting them to be quiet and polite even to that limited extent requires a fair amount of direct intervention, shouting, threats and last-resort bribes.)

As their children get older, many parents find them even more troublesome. Yes, the teenage years are difficult, but this is often overstated. Remember, you control the purse strings, and this is a very powerful position to be in. Then, when they hit 18, they are no longer your responsibility, so you can kick them out of the house and relax.

My four-year-old has become a walking embarrassment. Every trip to the supermarket is a nightmare, as he invariably points to some large woman and shouts, 'Mummy, look at that fat lady!' In the swimming pool last week, he went up to a rather unfit young man and demanded, 'Why have you got bosoms?' How can his tongue be curbed?
Mrs JF, Exeter

There is nothing you can do. It used to be misguidedly thought children were innocents: they are not. They are as conscious and morally aware as adults but choose not to reveal it. He is revelling in causing you maximum embarrassment. Wouldn't you enjoy being like him, speaking your mind without fear? Imagine being able to say to your pretentious sister-in-law, 'What hideous curtains', instead of making some glib compliment. Most people suppress this urge until they reach old age, when they pretend to be deaf and walk very slowly over zebra crossings to annoy motorists.

Please tell me how to cope with four kids, two mine and two my new companion's. I am about to call it all off and top myself. I hate it. It's depressing.
FO'H, Banbury

Call me irresponsible and lazy, but over the years I've come to the conclusion that giving each child a television and DVD set and computer terminal with unlimited Internet access means one rarely sees them, let alone hears from them. Bliss. Of course, there's every possibility they will grow up to be maladjusted social misfits with wasted bodies and an inability to concentrate for more than 30 seconds, but they could always become models.

I have a friend who has started to think that his children are exceptional. I can understand him being proud of them, but exceptional? I think not, especially when compared to my daughter. I feel he should be told the truth but with tact and sensitivity. Naturally, I thought of you. Can you help?
ETR, South Yorkshire

The truth should be brought home to him, but tact and sensitivity won't work. You need to impress corroborative evidence upon him. Arm yourself with all your daughter's school reports, swimming certificates, Brownie badges and so on. Then, when you next encounter him in the pub, or at a football match, you can simply pull out the relevant document and say, 'Ten yards front crawl. Match that.' Or, '"Lively imagination, always likes to contribute to lessons." They said less about Einstein.' He will soon get the message.

My friend and I were thrilled to be pregnant at the same time, but now she has annoyed me. She has had her baby boy three weeks early and given it exactly the name that I was planning to give mine. I want revenge.
TN, Birmingham

Carry on and give your child the name you were planning all along. Establish your friend's preferred version of the name, for, as you are no doubt aware, parents are passionate about this. Never use it when referring to her child. For instance, should the name be James, always call him Jimmy, and, when he's a bit older and they are friends, get your James to call him Jimmy, too. It will annoy her no end, but the child will eventually become known as Jimmy in perpetuity, or at least for the few months that you remain on speaking terms.

My parents don't understand me. They say I am letting them down. They hate the fact that I work in a bank and am happy to go off to work every day in a suit. They say I should be fighting the system, not shoring it up, and that when they were my age they were out on the streets demonstrating. Recently, I got engaged to a really super girl, and this seems to have pushed them over the edge. They are threatening to evict me. I protested that I would have nowhere to live, and they say I can move in with my fiancée, but I believe this would be wrong before we are married. (This attitude seems to infuriate them further.) How can I make peace with them?
MD, London NW3

The clash of generations is a fact of life, but don't worry too much: it's just a phase they're going through. They'll grow out of it. (You do sound a boring little toad, though.)

My husband believes that it's good for our children to suffer from aches and pains, as this may make them

more sympathetic when he is in pain. Is this a typical selfish male attitude or have I married an inhuman monster?
MGO, Anglesey

Your husband belongs to the 'character-building' school of child development, which likes to think of itself as non-interventionist, a kind of market-economy approach to child rearing. For example, if you say, 'Little Freddie has broken his arm. Shall I take him to the hospital?' your husband will reply, 'No, don't bother. It's character building.' Usually, however, they lack the courage of their convictions. If you say, 'Freddie wants a tutu for Christmas,' I guarantee his response will be, 'Bloody hell! Ring the child psychiatrist immediately.' He is a typical male: ignore him, as long as he is not trying to get your children to share in his hangovers.

My children are all making more money than I ever did, so there is now nothing more I can give them, let alone my grandchildren. I try giving them love, but they are too busy. I try giving them presents, but they can buy anything they want. Where have I gone wrong?
AG, Wilts

You have done everything right. You invested the best years of your life in your children, now it's payback time. The whole point of children is that they become successful and can keep you in more comfort than you ever knew earlier in your life.

The lives of two of our children have taken interesting turns. One has dropped out of university, and the other has 'come out'. Should I accept that these revelations are the responsibility of the parents or forget about it all and get on with refurbishing the utility room and the rest of our lives? I love them both dearly.
AW, Dorset

These things are both 'your fault' and 'nothing to do with you, I'm old enough to run my own life', depending on how it's going. So I wouldn't think too much about it, react accordingly as the occasion demands and get on with refurbishing the utility room.

I am now 60 years old but still wear jeans most days, have modern thoughts, wash my hair every day under the shower rather than visit the local hairdresser, and read books by Will Self. Is this why my children hate me?
AG, Wiltshire

Yes, try Julian Barnes or Ian McEwan instead.

We have been asked to contribute a list of possible names for imminent grandchildren. It has been stipulated that historical names are not appropriate for a person of the twenty-first century. Do you think Kaydot Taylor as a combined name and e-mail address is too modern?
TT, Bedford

No, just stupid. All names are of their time, so whatever you come up with will be an old person's name in 70 years' time. Agnes was once a racy eponym for bright young groovers, most Davids are now declining into middle age and, curiously, all Freddies are either over 75 or under 10. First names are very overrated. Mine is never used except by Mr Mills when he thinks he's at his most charming (actually, he's just wheedling).

My son's independence was short lived when a lady friend moved into his newly acquired bachelor flat. Do you think that in order to keep the predators at bay he should have emulated his Italian counterparts and stayed on living with his mama?
NAB, Oxford

Oh, come on. Ask yourself why he set up on his own in the first place. It's pretty difficult persuading sons to move out, but the prospect of rampant uninhibited sex will do it every time. Mothers can do most things for their sons, but this is one area, I think you'll find, they do best avoiding.

My two-and-a-half-year-old daughter has recently extended her vocabulary into unwelcome territory. This morning she found a rusty nail in the garden and exclaimed, 'What the bloody hell is this?' I am now worried that she is going to utter some obscenity at an inopportune time and that her foul-mouthed behaviour will reflect badly on me. What am I going to do?
Mrs AJC, Leeds

It could be worse. I had to pretend to my mother-in-law that her grandson had an inability to say the word 'fox' properly. Try praising her every time she says it, then, whenever you have a visitor, say, 'Go on, darling, show us how clever you are. What's your new word?' If she is anything like most children, she will refuse to say it for the rest of the day.

Please could you tell me how to open childproof bottles, jars, etc. when one's children have left home?
Mrs MLM, Preston

I think you'll find that once the children have left home, you suddenly don't need all those pills and medicines that you once took daily.

Since my mother, usually a placid woman, reached 50, there have been some extraordinary changes in her behaviour. I am especially concerned with her driving (the lack of gear changes and braking) and the ensuing bad language. How should I deal with her?
RS, Sutton Coldfield

It's just a phase. It happens to many women when they hit the half-century. I bet she's 'hanging out' with a bad lot, staying out till all hours dancing and 'knocking back' Babychams and brandy. She's probably planning to get her navel pierced and you could well find a packet of ten Marlboro Lights hidden in the bottom of her wardrobe. She'll grow out of it.

My husband is concerned that our son is developing what he calls an unhealthy interest in Judy Garland and Maria Callas. His room is devoted to these singers, full of books, recordings and posters. Should I be worried?
Mrs FE, Stevenage

No, but lock up your nail varnish and tell him to buy his own.

My daughter has done an Eliza Doolittle in reverse. She was carefully brought up and expensively educated, but her estuarine vowels, adopted at university, are excruciating. With Christmas coming and the imminent arrival of her grandmother from abroad, what can I do to prevent her having heart failure when confronted by this distressing condition?
MG, Cheltenham

Tell her grandmother that your daughter is keen to become an actress (rapidly becoming a respectable trade because of the money they can rake in). Your daughter will soon be auditioning for a part in a new play at the Royal Court (bound to have working-class people in it), and she wants to spend as much time as possible in character. As it will be Christmas, you could all join in the fun and pretend to be, say, a jolly East End family having a knees-up: mother gets maudlin drunk and dad threatens her with a slapping, daughter restrains him, all collapse in tears.

I am 18 years old and pregnant. When the baby is born, which surname should it have, mine or my boyfriend's? I am quite happy for it to be his, but my mum and dad are going bonkers and say that it should be mine, as we are not yet married. Is there any law on this, and what do you think is the right thing to do?
CH, Manchester

Who has got the better name, you or him? If your name is, say, Pratt, Bumleigh, Flabbicheeks or Git, then I would name the child after your boyfriend. Double-barrelled names are always best avoided, I think, especially in Manchester.

MRS MILLS SAYS The whole point of children is that they become successful and can keep you in more comfort than you ever knew earlier in your life.

Christmas

CHRISTMAS IS A TIME FOR FAMILIES – AND
therefore misery and a spike in the suicide rate. The
letters I have received over the years certainly bear this
out. I devised a short checklist to get everyone through
the festive season:

- BATTERIES: have every size and 12 of each, otherwise
  you will have weeping children clutching useless ray
  guns, static racing cars and speechless talking dolls.
  For your own sanity, make sure they have only half an
  hour of life left in them.

- TELEVISION: the biggest source of Christmas
  arguments, only soluble by having sets for every
  available channel. If this is not feasible, ensure that
  elderly female relatives are issued with plot cards
  for any film you plan to watch as a family. Thus their
  inevitable, repeated question – 'What's happening
  now?' – can be swiftly dealt with. These cards should
  also carry a schematic breakdown of the relationship
  of characters ('I thought he was her husband') and
  a filmography for the principal actors ('Wasn't he in
  Paint Your Wagon?').

- BULLYING AUNT: there will be one who will insist that the television is turned off and everyone plays games. Everyone should show enthusiasm and suggest Hide and Seek. When she has safely tucked herself out of sight (preferably in the garden), everyone gives up looking for her and returns to *Only Fools and Horses*.

- OTHER RELATIVES: it is always worth investing in alcohol at Christmas and giving them copious amounts. Lock the windows and turn the heating right up. They should wake up just in time to go home. (Always avoid serving boiled sprouts to elderly relations.)

- TURKEY: start cooking it on Christmas Eve and insist that your husband gets up every hour throughout the night to check it. This means that he will inevitably be awake to deal with the children when they leap out of bed at 4 a.m. You have previously insisted that you are on no account to be disturbed before 9 a.m. as you have so much cooking to do.

- VEGETABLES: their preparation is monotonous and repetitive. Make sure that your husband does them all on Christmas Eve, and they can sit on the hob in large pans of water. You, of course, have the more difficult task of preparing the pudding. (I always used to think one can never have too many sprouts. I was wrong.)

- THE PUDDING: the supermarkets do very good ones these days. Spend Christmas Eve destroying all evidence of the packaging.

- CHRISTMAS CARDS: sending them is a boring, pointless task. When December comes again, will anyone remember you didn't send a card last year? Inevitably a few will cross you off their list, but that's all right because you should never throw your cards away. Store them with your Christmas decorations and display them every year. Friends and relations will envy your popularity (and certainly be puzzled by it).

My sister-in-law has told me not to bother to buy her a Christmas present. She has bought one from me for herself, and her husband will wrap it on my behalf. All I need do, she informs me, is send her a cheque for £24.98. Should I bother?
AS, Manchester

Express your disappointment by saying that you had already bought her present. But tell her not to worry – she can regard it as her present to you as long as she sends you a cheque for £224.98.

What advice do you have for the hundreds of parents, like me, who have been unable to buy a Cyberman Helmet for their children? I am dreading facing my disappointed son on Christmas Day.
LJ, Warks

Buy him a dalmatian puppy instead. (Irony alert: dear RSPCA, this is not a serious suggestion.) You could tell him you donated the money to charity, though this would only fuel his anger and resentment: young children are so aggressively selfish and mean-minded that they would make wonderful executive chairmen. Pompous sentimentalism is a teenage trait. Anyway, I wouldn't worry too much: the helmet is not a proper toy. It doesn't even take over the brain. Children all over the country will be bored rigid by it come the new year, but at least their parents will feel less guilty slinging it into the nearest canal. Regard it as less of a problem and more of a lesson for life. Disappointment is always character forming. (© Platitudes of a Great British Childhood.)

As fairly new parents, we wonder whether we should continue to perpetrate the myth of Father Christmas with our three year old? Not only is it all rather old hat these days but we do rather strongly feel that children should never be lied to. What kind of values will it give them in later life?
Mrs JF, London N1

Children need to believe that a strange old man will clamber down the chimney in the middle of the night and sneak into their bedrooms. Just as they need to believe that crusts make their hair curly, carrots help them see in the dark, if they don't stay in bed the ferocious monster that lives in the bottom drawer will leap out and bite their heads off, and that daddy wasn't hurting mummy when she made that funny noise last night, he was just tickling her. They will grow up with the same values as the rest of us: knowing that a few fibs make life much more bearable.

Surely the most difficult character to buy presents for is the adolescent male. I cannot begin to comprehend what goes through the mind of my monosyllabic nephew, so buying him a gift is a nightmare. Do you have any suggestions?
Mrs TY, Solihull

How about a nice briar pipe and 4 oz of ready-rubbed tobacco? If he is not yet shaving (and you like him), buy him aftershave. Nothing flatters the ego of a teenage boy more, and, of course, it will last for months. If you don't like him, take the reverse tack and give him an Action Man or Pop-up Pirate game.

I like to think I am a generous sort, but often, when I have bought small, exquisite things, I feel that rather less knowledgeable relations dismiss them as small and therefore cheap. How do I subtly indicate their true value?
CM, Edinburgh

Always leave the price tags on.

I've stumbled across my present from my wife, and I hate it. Should I say something before Christmas Day?
CP, Lowestoft

Yes, but be subtle. Don't say, 'I hate pink golfing trousers.' Instead, slip it into conversation: for example, 'I saw Alan yesterday. His new pink golfing trousers are horrible.' If you receive the present regardless, draw your own conclusions.

The man next door has yet again covered his house with Christmas lights: a plastic sleigh with five reindeer in flashing neon adorns his roof, a fat Santa flashes on the porch and a jolly snowman illumines the front lawn. The whole effect is hideous. Would it be both churlish and snobbish to complain?
LC, Sutton Coldfield

Of course it would. Haven't you got an air rifle?

I am a 42-year-old man, yet every year my aunt still buys me a Christmas present appropriate for a boy of nine. In recent years, I have had Action Man outfits, Subbuteo teams, the *Beano* annual and bumper selection boxes of sweets. She may be in her dotage, but I still feel a bit of a charlie. Should I do anything?
CC, Brierley Hill

Retaliate. Buy her the Arctic Monkeys album and a silver ring for a pierced navel.

What is your recipe for the perfect Christmas?
VS, Liverpool

The three Ps: planning, planning and paying out large sums of money.

Having no family of my own, every Christmas is spent with my husband's. I have had enough and cannot bear to waste another festive day in their boring company. How can I avoid them without causing offence?
JH, Surrey

You should have written to me sooner, but here's a tip for next year. In early October, as the nights draw in, go into hibernation. The cupboard under the stairs is the best place. Fill it with straw, or torn-up newspaper, and withdraw into its cosy darkness until you feel the first stirrings of spring.

If my ageing great-aunt gives me one more china pomander this Christmas, I'll scream. I own 18 already. How can I let her know they're a bad idea without upsetting her? And what am I supposed to do with my collection of china balls? Their uses are limited.
Ms RC, London SW4

Pomanders have been given away at Christmas since 1586, when Elizabeth I invented them. Shame on you for rebelling against this yuletide tradition. Next, you'll be complaining about receiving the latest *Beano* annual and a selection box from great-uncle Joe. As for what to do with the china balls, that's easy: do what your great-aunt does and give them away as presents to undeserving nieces.

By the time I've finished stuffing my turkey, I don't much feel like eating it. Any suggestions?
Mrs E Good, Sheffield

Get your husband to stuff it for you. (He'll think it's Christmas.)

I have just received a letter from a pushy cousin in Chicago announcing that he and his family will be arriving in Britain on Christmas Eve. He expects me to

pick them up from the airport, and he wants to stay for a week. He knows we are spending Christmas at home, so I can't lie. How can I put him off convincingly?
JR, London SE23

As most Americans think our standard of living is unacceptably squalid (no air conditioning, small fridges and so on), write back exaggerating your domestic deprivation while assuring him of a warm welcome: for example, his family won't have to worry about underpowered British showers as you all scrub down in a tin bath in front of the kitchen fire; you may only have one lavatory, but privacy is not a problem as it's at the bottom of the garden. He might regard these as quaint attractions, so add that a local bylaw forbids the wearing of trainers, sneakers or any other form of leisure footwear over the Christmas period and that only sensible lace-ups are permissible.

My five-year-old daughter wants a horrible plastic Barbie accessory for Christmas, while I want to give her a first edition of *The Wind in the Willows*. What should I do?
ANM, London N8

Try to be less pretentious. Your relationship with your daughter will be much improved.

Is there a name for those people who dispatch all their Christmas cards, complete with their name and address, by (and never later than) 1 December?
MT, Shrewsbury

No, but there should be. Mr and Mrs Taylor would be my suggestion.

What's the best alternative to turkey for Christmas lunch?
Mrs FE, Cheam

Whatever else is on the restaurant menu.

My husband has invited an American business associate and his family to spend Christmas with us again. Last time they came, his table manners quite put me off my food – insisting on Diet Coke with his turkey and eating the brandy butter from the bowl with a spoon. How can I politely inform him that such things aren't acceptable in England?
SWL, Wilts

It would be rather pompous and an offence against one's duties as a hostess to start upbraiding guests for their failings, so I am afraid you must indulge them. However, ensure that you do not have proper Diet Coke but only Co-op Cola, Vimto or Tizer (there's no great reason for this, it's just annoying for them). They will, of course, be very keen to share in a traditional English Christmas, so after lunch you should introduce them to the old game of Hunt the Sixpence. You know the one: visitors to the house are required to retire from the table and to search the garden for a silver sixpence until it's past the children's bedtime, or hypothermia sets in (whichever is the sooner). Whether or not there actually is a sixpence hidden in the garden is entirely a matter for your conscience.

Unlike the way I was brought up, my sister-in-law's children receive all their presents first thing in the morning 'from Father Christmas', including the ones that I have bought for them. Why should someone else get the credit for the presents I have bought?
MM, Didsbury

Take the children to one side and explain to them that Father Christmas does not actually exist, that you bought the presents and their parents simply arranged them around the tree.

My husband said he wanted 'a waiter's friend' for Christmas. I'm baffled. I thought we had a good marriage. Can you advise?
BB, Sutton Coldfield

If that's what it takes to pop his cork, why not?

Is it acceptable for my 37-year-old husband still to insist on a stocking every year?
LF, Brightlingsea

Oh come on, why not? And I'd have thought that indulging him with stockings on his birthday and your wedding anniversary was a good idea, too.

Christmas is fast approaching, and our local cake shop is selling delicious iced gingerbread Santas. My wife and I have become quite addicted. However, whereas I nibble at the arms and legs, working my way towards the body, my wife just bites off the head, devours it, then discards the remainder. What does this betray of my wife's personality? Do you think there is some malicious intent on her part? Is our marriage in danger?
JL, Barry

Either her repressed sexual tensions have been sublimated into seeking expression in a simple, yet psychopathological, act of primeval significance, or she only likes the pink icing on the head. Both are common stages in the life of a woman.

I am dreading Christmas because of my four children. They become so completely overexcited that they stop sleeping properly, and two of them even start bedwetting again. They talk about what presents they are expecting all the time and turn the house upside down trying to find them. The sooner the day itself arrives and it's all over, the better. Is there anything I can do to calm them?
BJ, Lichfield

Don't wait, give in. Just say, 'OK, we'll have Christmas right now!' Dump all the presents on the kitchen table, put a Harry Potter film in the video and have cold

turkey for tea. You'll have a really miserable Christmas when 25 December actually arrives, of course, but it will teach your children a lesson they will never forget (and totally destroy all the magic, but this might be a price worth paying).

I am in a vague relationship with an extremely sexy, clever and funny guy who wants to sleep with me. For all the above reasons, I am not entirely sure why he wants to be with me. Is he using me? Do I actually mind (after all, he is really hot)? What on earth am I meant to give him for Christmas? I hope you can help me, as everyone else just tells me I shouldn't let myself feel pressured by him, or that I'm still underage, but he isn't pressuring me, and I will be 16 quite soon.
CC, Leeds

Give him socks and see if he still respects you the next day.

Christmas is coming and so is an annual dilemma. Every year, I send Christmas presents to my two brothers' children and every year they do not say thank you. Unless I ask their parents, I have no idea if the presents arrived in the post, were given to the children or if they liked them. I was brought up to sit down after Christmas with paper and pen and to 'do my thank-yous'. Good manners are usually taught by the mother, but my brothers' wives are not bothered. Should I say something or just keep quiet and accept it?
FR, County Wexford

It is entirely the parents' fault and therefore rather mean to deprive the children. Why not include a stamped addressed envelope and writing paper with the present? Doubtless your sisters-in-law will think you a patronising, self-righteous old bag, but you can't have it all ways.

Last Christmas, I sent my daughters and sons-in-law quite expensive presents. So far, they have done nothing, let alone thanked me. What should I do this Christmas?
AG, Wilts

Give them the same presents again. When they complain, say you assumed they didn't get them last year as they never thanked you. Better still, opt out of Christmas altogether. Take a cruise. Fly to New York on Concorde to go shopping. Announce your intention to spend all your assets before the grim reaper lays you low. They'll be all over you. It's manipulative and cheap but (let's face it) deeply gratifying. (I think I have said something similar to you before, AG. You are obviously ignoring my advice.)

I'm expected to go to Christmas dinner with my family. However, I have also been invited by my boyfriend's grandparents, who will be offended if I don't go, and brand me the ungrateful, irresponsible extension of their family. Bearing in mind that my boyfriend and I are expecting a baby, where should I go?
DW, Wales

Your boyfriend's family already think you are irresponsible for getting pregnant in the first place. I'd go home to mum.

Our Christmas guests (family) have told us they will be bringing their new karaoke DVDs to the festivities. The idea fills me with dread, as I sing in an amateur choir and am therefore seen as fair game. However, my voice is better suited to Brahms than Britney. How do I decline the microphone without appearing too condescending?
KM, by e-mail

Insist on supplying your own repertoire and perform the whole of Schoenberg's *Pierrot Lunaire*. That should put an end to their karaoke-based idea of fun.

What is the etiquette for dealing with Christmas carollers? When they sing 100 verses of 'O Come, All Ye Faithful', do you listen to the whole song, stop them halfway or shut the door on them? Also, how much are you expected to give?
JH, Kent

The recognised rate is £5 for the first verse, decreasing by £1 for each subsequent verse; more than five, they have to start paying you. Instead of money, you can offer homemade mince pies and a schooner of Emva Cream, which never fails to send them rapidly scooting off.

I am having a Christmas soirée, but all my friends have different food requirements. One is on a high-protein diet, one is doing low-GI and one has a wheat/gluten allergy. What is the right party food to serve in such a situation?
RM, London

Mulled wine.

As a woman of a certain age wanting to keep in shape, the thought of spending yet another Christmas slumped in front of the television, eating and drinking to excess, does not appeal. I should like to escape. I have a passport, money and no commitments, but where does a woman alone go to find congenial company?
CW, Berks

How should I know what you consider to be congenial company? Are you the kind of person who would rise to the challenge of a three-week intensive line-dancing course on a Greek cruise ship, or would you prefer hanging out with a biker gang perfecting wheelies on your Triumph Bonneville? Hitchhiking across North America might be interesting (take your own cutlery, though, as they don't use it, and I noted during Mr Clinton's videotaped evidence that they have now

given up on glasses, too, and drink straight from the can. Is there no end to their sloppiness?). The best place to meet people, apparently, is the supermarket, so now that many are open 24 hours a day, you could spend your entire Christmas there. (Believe me, it's better than line-dancing around the Aeolians.)

For years now I've been finding it difficult to hear the carol singing at my door when I'm watching recycled Morecambe and Wise Christmas Specials on television. As an ardent believer in old Christmas traditions, do you think I should ask the carol singers not to call? I would move the telly closer to the front door, but the cable isn't long enough.
MT, Shropshire

It is shocking what is being done to the traditional Christmas. Birmingham Council's renaming of the festival 'Winterval' to avoid upsetting other religions is the latest in a long line of official idiocies. However, there is good news. I can reassure you that during future Christmases, old Morecambe and Wise shows will be screened in churches throughout the land. Worshippers can thus enjoy the duo in rapt contemplation surrounded by fellow devotees, safe in the knowledge that there will be no irritating interruptions from religious singers or do-gooders collecting for charities. I for one am glad the Church has come to its senses and realised what Christmas is all about. The bishops would do well to remember that carols and religion are all very well but must be kept in their proper place. We don't want religion rammed down our throats, particularly at Christmas.

Over Christmas and the New Year, I suffered my own family as well as various in-laws. I am happy to see them about once every decade, but they seem to pop up each year. When gatherings are proposed in future, I would like to have some ready-made excuses for not joining in. Could you please provide me with a list of ten to give me some breathing space?
Mr SS, Hemel Hempstead

MRS MILLS SOLVES ALL YOUR PROBLEMS

1. 'I'm washing my hair.'
2. 'I can't leave the cat on its own.'
3. 'I'm having a fridge/sofa/small operating theatre delivered.'
4. 'I'll be ill.'
5. 'I'm cutting my toenails that night.'
6. 'I fell asleep in the bath/on the way to the kitchen.'
7. 'I thought you said June 25th, not December. Silly me!'
8. 'I got lost.'
9. 'I can't be bothered, but I'll pop over tomorrow to pick up my presents.'
10. 'It's funny but I feel nauseous whenever I am in the same room as you.'

MRS MILLS SAYS Christmas is a time for families – and therefore misery and a spike in the suicide rate.

How to Deal with the Wider World

Neighbours

'**Y**OU CAN'T CHOOSE YOUR RELATIVES', BUT YOU can move away from them. Neighbours are another matter: unless you are fortunate enough to live in a castle, there's always someone next door. And it seems that most of us have some kind of dispute going on with them.

Generally, it seems we are very suspicious of our neighbours and particularly enjoy spying on them. The net curtain was invented solely to make it easier for us to pursue this endlessly enjoyable pastime and the creation of Neighbourhood Watch schemes was absolutely inspired, giving us the perfect excuse to watch each other's houses and even poke about in them when the occupants are on holiday under the pretence that we are 'keeping an eye on things' for them.

One of the primary functions of neighbours is to make us feel better about ourselves. Social scientists claim that contentment lies in being richer than those who live around you. It is unimaginative to complain that this can only be possible for a few people, as obviously the majority of the street must perforce be less well off. There are a hundred ways to be richer than other people. The key is to unleash your inner snob. I sneer at the man across the road for having a Porsche Cayenne rather than a reliable, understated, family-friendly old Volvo estate. He jeers at me for driving a wreck. We laugh at the family who festoon the outside of their house with Christmas lights; they pity our children for having such killjoy parents. We loathe the couple who listen to 1980s pop music in their garden all summer; they haven't forgiven us for the Bonfire Night extravaganza we organised that traumatised their shitzu. And so it goes on. Yet we count ourselves a happy, close-knit little community.

Noise, nudity, unsuitable washing on the line, windchimes, dogs, fencing – there is no aspect of life that people won't disagree about. Of course, most of the time I could say, 'Well, pop round and have a word with your neighbour and I'm sure you can sort it out together.' But this is Britain. People would rather eat raw baby rats than raise a difficult, potentially embarrassing matter. In fact, not only would they be prepared to chow down on rats rather than talk, they would also torch their neighbour's car, put his windows through and dynamite his lawn. Which is where I can come in with other constructive suggestions . . .

My neighbour persists in allowing her small dog to foul the corridor outside my front door. I have no reason to believe that I have antagonised her in any way, but I feel I must put a stop to this and, at the same time, try to avoid a personal confrontation for the sake of good neighbourliness. I have thought of (a) poisoning her dog, (b) transferring its deposits to its owner's front door, (c) buying a large dog myself. Can you think of anything better?
MMC, Gibraltar

You are right about preserving good neighbourliness, so pop round to discuss it with her over a cup of tea. Before entering her flat, however, make sure that you have firmly trodden in her dog's latest deposit and thus leave traces of it smeared all over her shagpile. This manoeuvre should focus her mind on the seriousness of the matter.

Our neighbour has erected a six-foot fence just one yard from our house, and, naturally, we are none too keen on the new view. We have considered suffering in silence, making our feelings plain and setting fire to the fence in the wee small hours. Which would you recommend?
FR, Anstruther, Fife

Call a glazier and have a large window fitted in it.

The chap whose garden backs onto ours has planted a row of quick-growing conifers. They are not particularly attractive trees and, in a couple of years, will block most of the sunlight from our garden. He is by no means a reasonable man. Is there an easier answer than dragging in lawyers?
DB, Croxley Green

Buy a pet beaver.

We live in a quiet cul-de-sac of genteel, semi-detached bungalows on the outskirts of a seaside town. Recently, an extraordinarily pretty air hostess bought one and moved her lover-boy in with her. They make love at all hours, and their bedhead bangs against my 90-year-old mother's party wall. She thinks the screams are because the man is beating her up. Should I get the local authority noise-abatement people to intervene? A neighbour tried to remonstrate, but she was told to f*** off. What are we to do to ensure a good night's sleep or, indeed, afternoon's nap?
MC, South Coast

You could retaliate by playing 'Je t'aime' at loud volume, although, if the air hostess believes that your 90-year-old mother is the perpetrator of those moans it might prove a little too alarming for her. Better would be to play a recording of persistent, infectious laughter. In my experience, the merest hint of a snigger is enough to put people off their stroke.

On the first morning in my new flat, I emerged onto the communal veranda in braces accompanied by my tabby cat. Later that day, my neighbour complained that my dishabille was 'not customary' and said that my cat was common. 'I just thought I would mention these matters,' she added. I have been wondering ever since how to proceed. I am prepared to put a pullover over my braces, even in the hottest weather, but how about the cat, to which I am deeply attached?
ART, East Sussex

Obviously your neighbour does not want you to 'lower the tone', as she would no doubt phrase it. So you must watch your step. First of all, don't wear a pullover. Get a football shirt instead. They are ever so trendy and come in lovely bright shiny colours. Try Manchester United, Newcastle or even England. As for the cat, she is right: single tabbies are common, but not two, so get it a mate, or better (i.e. rarer) still, pair it up with a friendly dog – a rascally pit bull terrier, for instance. If she says anything after that, you can always reply cheerily, 'Oi, button it, missis, or he'll have your leg off.'

Why is it that people who feed stray cats do so below someone else's window? Since I do not fancy putting up with a cat serenade when my neighbour finally decides to call it a day, what strategies should I adopt to dissuade her?
NS, Nottingham

What on earth are you going on about? I have never encountered this phenomenon. The only explanation is that your neighbour wants to annoy you. Dispatch the cat with a shotgun. If your neighbour is hysterically distraught, then you can be sure she was not trying to irritate you but was just a bit strange about her choice of feline feeding venue. What a relief that will be, as it would be awful to find out one's neighbours didn't like one and were trying to be tiresome.

I always look forward to seeing a spinster friend of mine when I visit my holiday flat because she soon brings me up to date with the general goings-on. This year, she seemed quite distressed because some new neighbours were regularly sunbathing in the nude on their patch. As far as I could gather, the couple in question were quite secluded, and I told her so. Do you think my friend was probably standing on a chair more often than not?

Fl, Bristol

Of course she was. You should have a quiet word with those neighbours and ask them to move. Having to stand on a chair is obviously upsetting your friend, so it would help if the sunbathers moved to make it easier for her to see them. It is often thought spinsters are particularly prone to prurience, but in fact it affects many women as they reach *une certaine age* (a certain age). Any photographs?

As you can see from our address and the quality of writing paper, we are a respectable family. Our problem is our neighbour, a single gentleman working in the City who never has any visitors to his home. Of late he has started doing his washing on a Sunday. The usual gentlemen's garments appear on the washing line along with three pairs of ladies' knickers (frilly). We have never experienced this sort of behaviour in the past. My husband thinks I should go round and speak to the young man about it. Could you please give me some tips?

Mrs DR-J, East Sussex

I'm not sure I understand the problem. Do you think three pairs of knickers too few and therefore evidence of unhygienic habits in the underwear department of his life? Or have you realised after all these years that your neighbour is a bit kinky and therefore it might be mutually beneficial if you were to get to know him better? Please clarify.

Your correspondent Mrs DR-J of Sussex says she has a problem because her bachelor neighbour hangs out frilly knickers with his weekly washing. What is her problem? A very high proportion of the men Mrs DR-J encounters during a normal day will also be wearing frilly, lace or chiffon knickers. They are more comfortable, much prettier and more sensual than those intended for men. Why should women have all the fun?
IJ, Colwyn Bay

Quite so, Mr J. The reverse is also true, of course. I'd have been lost on several occasions had it not been for my stout Y-fronts keeping out the cold.

My next-door neighbour is driving me mad. She copies everything I do – new clothes, hairstyle, home furnishings and items for the garden. I know imitation can be viewed as a form of flattery, but enough is enough. How can I call her bluff?
Mrs PJH, Berks

We have a nice, shiny Volvo; our neighbour has a rusting 1970s Datsun. Our house has just been painted blue; our neighbour's was painted lime green 27 years ago. Our front garden has a magnificent rhododendron just about to flower; our neighbour keeps two spare cars in his that haven't been on the road in the past decade. We like the later trios of Beethoven; our neighbour likes Motorhead. When a window gets broken, we like to have new glass put in; our neighbour likes to use brown tape and cardboard. So stop moaning.

My neighbour has put up ghastly bamboo wind chimes in our joint porch. She thinks it is 'good feng shui'. I think it is noise pollution. How should I deal with it?
JL, Cheam

Buy a panda.

How can I tell my neighbours that their front garden is more appropriate to a council estate than a conservation area? Serried rows of antirrhinums, lobelia and bulk-bought daffodils tied up in knots have me spitting teeth. I offered to plant up a section for them, but they just say they will think about it. How do I bring them into this century with their gardening without hurting their feelings? With all the excellent gardening programmes on television and advice in publications such as yours, is there any excuse for this? It is lowering the tone of the entire neighbourhood.
Mrs NS, Ashford, Kent

Any comment would be extremely rude and upsetting, so either you must be prepared to be regarded as an outrageous snob who believes in certain standards and says so whether it hurts people or not, or you can remain quiet, reasonable and friendly. By the way, your writing paper is unbelievably naff. If this choice of paper – a fluffy cloudscape on a pale blue background with an abstract dove of peace flapping across a yellow sun – is indicative of your general level of taste, I am not surprised your neighbours are reluctant to let you loose on their herbaceous borders.

When the weather is hot, I like to take a little streak in my neighbours' swimming pool while they are away. They are not aware of it, as I do not upset their alarm systems, security cameras, etc. But the pool is often green with algae. How can I get them to keep it clean without raising suspicions?
Ms KR, Birmingham

Invariably the man deals with security, so your course of action is obvious. Make sure one of the cameras is trained on the pool as you ply your naked lengths. When finished, push yourself out of the pool, pausing half out of the water, allowing it to stream in rivulets over your toned cleavage, then towel yourself vigorously before the camera. You'll find that the pool will be kept in sparkling condition thereafter.

Our neighbour, a former footballer, cannot kick the spitting habit. How can we stop him?
WA, Wakefield

Try using a whistle. Some former players are so befuddled after years of heading the ball that they have lost touch with reality and think the whole of life is a football game. I saw one former hard-man centre-half approached by an old lady heading for the post office. She tried to sidestep him, but he brought her down with a sliding tackle and booted her shopping basket down to the greengrocers. Three people leapt to restrain him, and he became convinced he must have just scored. (He is now trying to break into commentating on the grounds that he is one of the few people in the country who knows what Ron Atkinson is talking about.) So give a short blast on a whistle and say, 'A quiet word, son: any more of that and you'll be off.'

MRS MILLS SAYS Noise, nudity, unsuitable washing on the line, windchimes, dogs, fencing – there is no aspect of life that people won't disagree about.

On the Domestic Front

PROPERTY HAS BECOME THE NATIONAL SPORT. Acres of newsprint are given over to covering it, specialist magazines are pushed through the letterbox and television stations run programmes throughout the day and into the night on buying it, improving it, selling it and buying it again. So 'homecare' has become a vital issue, not I suspect because 'it makes a house a home' but more as a way of protecting and enhancing your investment.

I have come to the view that rather than making life more comfortable, excessive 'homecare' actually makes houses unliveable, sterile environments. Everyone seems to want their house to look as if a designer has just finished with it, so the kitchen will look wonderful, but nothing will ever be cooked in it for fear of damaging the twinkling surfaces or disturbing the symmetrical arrangement of saucepans. No sentimental tokens litter a mantelpiece, only a solitary gerbera in an Italian vase. No broken-backed book at the side of a collapsed but comfortable armchair, only a neat chronological pile of design magazines by a Dutch constructivist 'lounger'. So, rather than passing on red-hot tips for getting red wine out of nappies or lifting diesel stains out of a bedroom carpet, I find myself having to tell correspondents to revise their expectations of what constitutes perfection in the home.

This is just as well as modern cleaning products are so superefficient that all that know-how concerning soda crystals, torn-up pieces of brown paper, bits of sisal and a judicious dab of hydrochloric acid ('and then hang the trousers at the end of the garden overnight') has gone by the board anyway.

Of course, there is a lot of curiosity about the Mills' household, and I am constantly refusing the blandishments of glossy magazine editors to feature it in a series of sumptuous colour spreads. It's not that I am terribly precious, just that I mind the thought of strangers poking their noses into my private space. I cannot claim that my approach to interior décor is startlingly original: I have a few fundamental tenets, but I know a great many English families have followed the same path. It is now regarded as a style when actually it's avoidance of having to do anything as disruptive as decorating or indeed tidying up too often. Wallpaper is terrific. Buy the most expensive you can afford in classic patterns, such as William Morris, and you can avoid having to redecorate for decades. Fitted carpets are to be avoided. They look terrible when they wear. Loose Turkey carpets, on the other hand, improve with wear and age, and gain in character. Never have an en suite bathroom. (It's like living in a hotel.) Double glazing is ridiculous. I know people claim that it can reduce heating bills and save the environment, but that only applies to those vulgarians who have their central heating switched on apart from December and January anyway. It is obscene to see people wandering about their houses in T-shirts in the winter months, why do they think God invented tweed and woollen underwear? Finally, remember, books can furnish a room, but an armchair is easier to sit on.

What colour should we paint our bedroom?
Mrs IF, Willenhall

Cornflower blue.

Whatever happened to spring cleaning? Nobody seems to do it any more.
Mrs SD, Clacton

Spring cleaning was abolished, along with spring itself, when the water companies were privatised and it was decided the seasons would run from dry winter to summer drought with no intervening showery period.

I have a large, slightly decrepit old house that I bought five years ago as a challenge for my old age. The challenge has proved rather more than I can cope with. I've done most things, but further problems keep asserting themselves, and it's all very expensive. Should I keep going, or sell and get out?
AG, Wilts

People these days have ridiculously high expectations of houses. They really believe that windows should be draughtproof, central-heating systems should provide enough hot water for a deep bath and roofs should not leak. All a lot of whimpering nonsense. An English home, like English clothes and dogs, should rot nobly about its owners. So, invest in some extra woollies and sensible underwear and put up with it.

My sister-in-law pontificates all the time on the superiority of her domestic cleaning methods. Neither her cleaner nor I come within miles of her sky-high standards. Casting a jaundiced eye at my picture-laden walls, she announced that she thoroughly dusts the backs of her pictures every two weeks, adding that this is why she does not have many pictures. I am toying with the idea of turning all my pictures to the wall, thus ensuring that the backs will bear inspection. The trouble is, I am wondering how my friends will react to this, as we are all in our seventies now and some are of a nervous disposition. Please advise.
P, Manchester

Cleanliness may be next to godliness, but it is also, as your letter shows only too well, disturbingly close to madness. As long as it is not a health risk, I never worry too much about tidiness. A bit of dirt only boosts the immune system, I always say, though rotting smells and anything quietly fermenting in a corner are best dealt with sooner rather than later.

Is it acceptable to have an untidy house when you have visitors? If not, how do you cope when guests pop round unannounced?
DP, Great Yarmouth

As the old proverb has it, 'Tidy house, depraved mind'. If you really wish to avoid unexpected visitors, follow the example of Mr Mills and me and hide under the kitchen table – not that we always need the excuse of visitors.

Whenever it is wet and I go out into the garden, I seem to end up treading on snails. How can I avoid them?
LJ, London

I wouldn't bother.

I like to have a clean and tidy house but hate doing housework. I am too mean to pay someone else to do the cleaning and wondered, as you appear to be a superwoman managing both a career and a home, if you know any handy hints for getting the chores done quickly while having fun at the same time?
Mrs PJ, Slough

Every time you feel your house has fallen from your preferred standards of tidiness, put it up for sale and move. I am afraid the only joy in housework is to regard it as an end in itself and not simply as a means to an end, as Kant remarked. In his own way, I like to think, Ruskin elaborated on this in *Fors Clavigera*. Extensive reading of these two thinkers should bring

you to a proper appreciation of dusting the picture rail twice a month, polishing those funny grey knobs on the radiators and vacuuming under the bath. I am flattered that you call this a career. I only do it to be able to afford my cleaning lady, Lyudmilla.

My husband's aunt has given us a hideous vase. It's far too big to lose in our cramped cupboards and I am not keeping it in the wardrobe to whip out on the (far too frequent) occasions that she visits. What can I do with it?
TG, Hendon

I'll lend you Lyudmilla for the afternoon: that should do it. (If you have any fragile ornaments you do like, however, I suggest you pack them up and store them in a safe place for the day, next door if possible.)

Some time ago you hinted that your hard-working cleaning lady sometimes did not handle your cherished possessions with sufficient care. Since then we have been keenly anticipating an update. Did this luckless lady hand in her notice: (a) on that Sunday as a result of reading your column in her copy of *The Sunday Times*? (b) on the following Monday as a result of reading your copy of the paper while relaxing on your chaise longue? (c) on the following Tuesday when she noticed your column while using an old newspaper to line the bottom of your parrot cage?
PCWB, Bristol

None of the above. It was, in fact, the following Friday, when she emerged from the lavatory wearing a hurt expression and clutching the offending scrap of paper, which had been hanging from a nail on the back of the door.

I have this friend who I visit quite a lot. Recently, he moved in with his girlfriend. Although she is quite a pleasant lady, she has what appears to me to be an

obsession with tidiness and cleanliness. How she runs her own home is her concern, but she now asks me (and other guests) to remove our shoes before we enter the living room. I find this a bit much, and I would like to know whether it is generally considered improper to make such a demand of guests to one's home.
RG, Huddersfield

It is shockingly bad form (although it is just as bad to turn up with dirty footwear). Next time you go round, make sure you have not washed your feet or changed your socks for a fortnight beforehand. As you leave (probably shortly after you've arrived, if your feet are cheesy enough), mention that it is such a pleasure to remove your shoes when you have rampant verrucas and athlete's foot.

My wife and I are redesigning our kitchen. Being careful sort of people, we have not scrimped on planning this important capital project. There is not a quality DIY or home-improvement magazine that we have not studied most thoroughly. However, one matter baffles us: where do those folk whose kitchens and sculleries are featured keep their washing-up liquid? In not a single kitchen photograph do we see a soapy container on a ledge behind a sink. Can you help?
MB, Dublin

How sweetly naive you are. You are behind the times in Dublin because no person of taste cooks in the kitchen any more. You don't spend all that money on a kitchen just to get it mucky. Suppose something spilt on the gleaming stainless-steel hob or burnt one of those tin-lined copper pans hanging over the pristine butcher's block? Perhaps I ought to explain that the most sumptuous houses featured in those magazines, owned by the most fashionable people, are not even actually lived in (cream shagpile was never meant to be walked on, nor muslin curtains ever drawn). I'm sure Ireland will catch up with the beau monde soon.

My personal domestic nirvana is currently disrupted by a dispute of epic proportions. My girlfriend and I are the proud owners of a magnetic strip on the kitchen wall for placing our extensive collection of kitchen knives upon. She maintains that these knives should be placed point up with the handle downwards. I disagree: the point must surely be downwards with the handle at the top to prevent the heavier knives sliding off. Various erudite books, including Delia, have failed to enlighten us. Please help.
NP, Letchworth

Throw it away and buy a knife block.

Why do men get into so much trouble from women for failing to put the loo seat down?
RM, London E1

Because, despite what they might think, the world is not run for their convenience.

Why do we say 'Wipe your feet' when we really mean 'Wipe your shoes'?
BO, Luton

I thought about this question for a long time and even considered getting up, walking across the room and consulting my groaning shelf of reference books, but then I realised I don't really care.

Recently, I popped home unexpectedly to find my cleaner (who is male and an absolute treasure in most respects) pottering about the house in my new Manolo Blahnik shoes. I pretended not to notice. When I next put on the shoes – previously a touch too tight – they were noticeably more comfortable. I have several other pairs that would benefit from this treatment. Do you think it would be in order to ask him to wear them for a short spell while he makes with the Mr Sheen?
SF, Wolverhampton

Absolutely not. Give in on shoes and there's no telling where it will end. You'll probably come home one afternoon and find him feather dusting your pelmets wearing nothing but your Agent Provocateur underwear and a silly grin. And you won't want that sagging round your bottom.

Any hints on removing moths from fur coats?
AG, Edinburgh

The only sure way of keeping clothes free of moths is to wear them, although with a fur coat you should carry an aerosol can of Doom mothproofing spray in the pocket – not for the coat but for warding off attacks by wild-eyed animal liberationists. It is available from the larger branches of Boots.

**MRS MILLS
SAYS**

Books can furnish a room, but an armchair is easier to sit on.

Work

WORK OCCUPIES SUCH A LARGE CHUNK OF OUR lives. Schooldays seemed to go on for ever and occupy a privileged place in most people's memories. It is therefore disturbing for many when they realise they have been turning up and working in the same place with the same bunch of people for three or four times as long as they were at school.

Any number of Germans have theorised about work. Hegel considered its importance in creating the identity of the individual, while Marx saw the alienation of labour as one of the besetting sins of the capitalist system. In Britain, on the other hand, we tend to be more relaxed in our attitude towards it. We regard work as quite a good thing, as it gets us out of the house and gives us something to do during the day, but we don't like to be seen to be too enthusiastic about it and manage just to do enough to get by while looking forward to our next holiday.

I had a number of jobs in my younger days: all of which I hated. I worked in the postroom of a multinational company where I was constantly berated by my colleagues for working too efficiently, thus giving ourselves nothing to do for most of the day. Working in a shop only gave one a growing contempt for the rest of humanity. Farmwork was backbreaking and mind-numbingly repetitious. All offices turned out to be staffed by eccentrics only moments away from being certified as insane: I remember one man, head of purchasing, who was obsessed with green. Everything he wore was green, his stapler was green, his phone was green, his briefcase was green. I can safely say it was one of the most unsettling encounters of my life and has given me a lifelong aversion to green. The rest of the office had worked alongside him for so long they no longer saw just how jaw-droppingly bonkers he was.

It is not surprising that letters about work turn out not to be about work but about our old favourite, human relations, although in that fascinating environment, the workplace. The social dynamics of the workplace are a rich source of comedy and terror, from the office lecher to the hopelessly inadequate boss thrashing about making everyone's life a misery.

Apparently Britons start planning for their retirement earlier than any other nationality. I am not at all surprised.

Day after day, I willingly put myself in the position of being mocked by my superior in the office. What started as a simple desire to please has deteriorated into a twisted exchange of diabolical insults and slights on my character. Is there any way I can resolve the situation?
CM, Kilburn

Here we have what Nietzsche derived from Hegel and called the 'master–slave relationship'. Unfortunately, you are the slave and there is an ineluctable, world-historical inevitability to your miserable position, i.e. deep down you are a squirming little worm and stuck with it. Sorry about that.

I think my boss fancies me. I haven't been working for him for very long, but every day when he arrives, he makes a point of saying 'Good morning', which he never does to anyone else in the office. Already, he

is asking me to stay behind to do extra work, such as retyping letters I did earlier in the day because they had the tiniest spelling mistake in them that nobody else would notice. Often, he interrupts what I am doing – even when I am talking on the phone to my mum – and tells me to come into his office to take some dictation. Yesterday, he made me work through my lunch hour to catch up on some filing that did not seem in the least bit urgent to me, and he sat at his desk without doing a thing to help, just ogling me, I suspect. Whenever I ask him if I can leave early, he rolls his eyes and sighs very suggestively as if he is upset that we are parting. I tremble at the thought of him making a move, as I know he is a married man. What shall I do?
ST, London

Sadly, I fear that your boss will be forced to let you go to place temptation beyond his reach.

I recently changed jobs, leaving the office where I had worked for 17 years. My former colleagues all clubbed together and presented me with a garishly fake leopard-skin car-seat cover. What am I to make of this bizarre gift?
Mrs DL, Basingstoke

They never liked you. Leopard-skin car-seat covers have not been manufactured since 1973.

Recently, I left a job where I like to think I developed close and lasting contacts with my colleagues. Imagine my shock and distress when I recently heard that one of them was giving a large garden party to which she was inviting seemingly half the world but not me. I am naturally upset and wonder what I can have done wrong. Or was I deluding myself about the harmony of our working relationship?
WH, London

For goodness' sake, woman. It is not a large garden party but a select gathering of smart sophisticates and

urbane men of affairs (plus a few of Mr Mills' friends) for cocktails. I would have thought it was blindingly obvious why you weren't invited. (I hope you have made good use of your leaving present. You'll find that not only are unpleasant smells banished, but your shoes will last longer, too.)

We have a gym as part of our office complex. It is cheap and obviously very convenient. The only drawback is always encountering work colleagues. What is the etiquette when one is sweating away next to Linda from accounts or George from senior management?
JHG, London

In many gyms, the common practice is the briefest acknowledgement of acquaintance, a nod of the head or quick smile. This is really rude. We should all be much more friendly. Good opening lines for conversation might be: 'I'd never have guessed that you came here', 'Keep at it, you've still got quite a bit to lose', 'You don't sweat much for a fat girl.' Always lean over their machines and point out how slowly they are running or what an abysmally low level they have set on the cycling machine; such encouragement will always be welcomed and make you a popular figure.

I have recently been the subject of vicious office gossip centring on a perfectly innocent incident in a lavatory with a colleague that actually took place several months ago. What can I do to stop my co-workers talking about me in this rather tedious fashion? My husband is becoming increasingly annoyed.
OM, London N5

There is nothing whatsoever that can be done to stop colleagues gossiping. Consequently, my view has always been that one might as well give them something juicy to gossip about.

I have recently joined the health club at work, where I swim every day before going back to the office. Unfortunately, I find colleagues engage me in conversation in the locker room to discuss stodgy committee meetings and budget targets. I feel disconcerted when they strike up during my shower or in my transition from Calvin Klein underwear to Speedos and back again. How do I handle these interactions when I am focused on my physical rather than my intellectual agility?
DWF, London

Maintain the focus on the physical and say, for example, 'Race you over three lengths to decide whether it's three redundancies or four in your department', or 'Do 70 sit-ups in a minute and your budget cut will only be 2.5%.' Colleagues will soon avoid you.

My immediate boss at work is often extremely grumpy. He is inclined to be a bit stiff and stand on his dignity. He doesn't really mix with the rest of us or join in the usual office banter. I usually have to work quite closely with him and find it a bit of a downer when he is in a bad temper. Is there anything at all I can do to buck him up and generally improve relations?
BGH, London

It is most important that when he seems depressed you should not allow him to infect your good mood. Be ebullient and cheer him up. Slap him on the back, ruffle his hair and say, 'Cheer up, misery guts, it might never happen.' Do impressions of well-known soap stars and ask him to guess which ones they are. He'll thank you for it in the end. Believe me.

MRS MILLS SAYS

In Britain, we regard work as quite a good thing, as it gets us out of the house and gives us something to do during the day.

Out and About

TRAVEL IS EASIER AND CHEAPER THAN IT HAS
ever been, although not in parts of the Middle East, and
the budget airlines don't appear to be in any rush to open
routes to Afghanistan (which isn't helping the market in
holiday homes for property-hungry Britons).

Travel is both the blessing and the curse of modern
life. A blessing because it has expanded the gene pool and
stopped us having six fingers and poor eyesight; a curse
because it has shrunk the world. Thailand used to be an
exotic destination known only to romantic sailors and
shifty adventurers, now it's a student stopover, drained
of mystery and as alluring as Glastonbury in a damp
summer. Yet everyone remains so boringly competitive
about their 'travelling' (the word holiday is usually
avoided these days). The usual boasts are vast distances
travelled in the shortest possible time ('So we got off the
ferry, drove through the night and were on the slopes the
next morning') and spots that no one else knows about
('Yes, it's a little trattoria right in the middle of Florence,
but apart from us there were only locals', 'Remarkably we
had the whole island to ourselves, apart from the locals
obviously, most of whom appeared thinly disguised in
Captain Corelli's Mandolin').

The modern tourist is caught in a paradox that would
surely have stimulated the philosophers of classical

tragedy. He wants an unspoilt, authentic experience, but he wants to get there easily and cheaply (and he doesn't want to be ripped off on car hire either). His arrival can only destroy his dream. Sometimes I think it would be more honest to spend two weeks on the Costa del Sol drinking lager and eating fry-ups, but five seconds later I come to my senses and decide to spend another summer trying to find the perfect French village where the locals play boules and sip pastis while force feeding geese and stirring the bouillabaisse, and English hasn't been heard since the Plantagenets left.

However, as I realised a few years after leaving university, life isn't all holiday. Alongside the letters about lost luggage, sending postcards and surviving in desert conditions, I receive sheaves about negotiating footpaths, lost front-door keys and motoring. I have included them here on the grounds that they are connected with travelling in the broadest sense: that is, they take place in the great beyond on the other side of the front door.

Whenever I'm walking along a pavement and someone is coming towards me, I always veer to the wrong side as they approach, thereby triggering an elaborate dance routine. Did my parents omit something crucial from my upbringing? Is there a correct side to stick to, as on London Underground escalators, or is there no 'proper' way of doing this?
BA, London NW3

I dealt with a similar problem some months ago. In that case, it was the repression of subconscious aggression linked with overdeveloped territorial possessiveness, manifesting itself in the constant barging of other people out of the way. In your case, it is clearly your parents' fault. You are overcompensating for a lack of affection in childhood by desperately seeking physical contact with strangers, no matter how fleeting. Carry a cuddly toy around with you and the urge to brush against passers-by will vanish.

While walking in Newquay town centre yesterday, I thought I saw my friend Peter across the road, but when I went over it wasn't him. Should I keep looking?
BD, Newquay

This happens a lot in Newquay, Bournemouth and other coastal towns with a concentration of bungalows near the sea front. Look on the bright side: at least this search gives you a purpose in life.

I have just started work in Namibia quite close to the desert, where water is in short supply. In which order should I see to my daily needs to make best use of my weekly water ration?
HT, Namibia

Drink it first. Wash in it afterwards. It never works the other way around.

I am frequently assaulted in my local supermarket by women wielding shopping trolleys. Is this a subtle form of introduction or indicative of the need for a driving test for female trolley operatives?
PEW, Alton

Prolonged observation of the progress of trolleys around supermarkets shows that women never bump into other women, only men. This is because it is the men who don't know what they are doing. Women know the layout of their local supermarket so well they can draw up their shopping lists in the order by which the items will be taken from the shelves; they could shop with their eyes closed. Imagine their irritation at some male zigzagging hither and yon, covering 15 times as much ground as he needs to as he goes from the fresh veg to the lager, then back for the olive oil without picking up the loo rolls en route. Your letter is typical presumptive male arrogance, Mr W. You are being assaulted but still fail to get the message.

If all roads lead to Rome, how come the A148 ends in Cromer?
CS, Hertford

Because that's where it starts from.

In order to avoid offence, I dispatch postcards to all and sundry while on holiday, thus restricting my time to relax and enjoy myself. In your opinion, who warrants a card and what should one say?
ED, Egypt

PS Having a lovely time. Wish you were here. Weather's fine.

In these days of telephones, postcards are almost redundant. Does anyone you care about not know you are in Egypt? But postcards still have one advantage. Because only the briefest of messages are possible from faraway places, they are perfect for dealing with sticky situations. Thus, to your boyfriend, for example, you might write: 'Having a lovely time. Glad you're not here, as have decided to dump you. Please post my spare underwear through letterbox.' Or to a junior colleague at work: 'It's gorgeous here. Living it up in five-star luxury. Don't bother going in to the office next week, you've been fired. Personnel have put your P45 in the post. Weather fabulous.'

Why is it that my front door key is always in the last pocket I feel in? Starting my search with the last pocket does not help. I have thought of putting my clothes on back to front but fear this would complicate my life even further. Can you help?
TH, Coventry

Don't be so silly. Get real and do what the rest of us do: have duplicate front door keys in every pocket.

Having just retired, my wife and I are thinking of taking a cruise. However, the thought of not being able to get

off the ship immediately if the need arose, or having to put up with a persistent pest on board, is making us think twice. How can we overcome our fears?
AC, Northampton

Wear a life belt at all times. Then, should some dreadful bore start droning on, simply toss yourself over the side.

It would be so pleasurable to have one's holiday wardrobe with one on holiday. Apart from carrying it as hand luggage and never transporting culinary spices, is there anything more one can do to win the love and respect of Heathrow baggage handlers? Would travelling first class make a difference?
JA, Ripon

It took me a while to work out what your letter was going on about at first, as I envisaged you struggling to the check-in desk with an awkwardly shaped piece of mahogany furniture. Then I realised that you were simply complaining about the frequency with which airlines lose luggage. There is no easy solution. I know that lots of show-offs boast that they manage to take everything as hand luggage, but it is not always practical. Usually these selfish people are, in fact, taking on ridiculously large bags and gambling that the cabin crew will shy away from confrontation. They then jam their enormous holdalls into the overhead locker, leaving no room for the modest handbags of others. Were I to be an air hostess, I would eject such 'hand luggage' at 30,000ft over the Atlantic while encouraging the rest of the passengers to hum the *Dambusters* theme. I have yet to find an answer to guaranteeing one's luggage always arrives at the same destination. Perhaps, inadvertently, you are right, and the answer lies in travelling with an actual wardrobe, conspicuous and difficult to misplace. I shall try it this summer. (Useful tip: a solid piece of Victorian joinery will probably be better than a flat-packed self-assembly vinyl-covered MDF unit from IKEA.)

While discussing travel, someone accused me of being merely a tourist, whereas he claimed to be a traveller. What exactly did he mean?
MA, Cardiff

That he felt himself to be your social superior.

I am the owner of a Rover P4. Recently, however, in my dreams I have been driving a Rover P5. What does this say about me?
JDM, London N8

That you sleep alone.

I write to you in despair. As a frequent flyer, I often have the misfortune to be seated directly behind rather large ladies or gentlemen. I find this inconvenient to say the least. On my last flight, a person sat in front of me and the seat inclined an alarming six inches back towards me, without them touching the recline button! Could you please tell me what I should do to make my flights more comfortable?
NM, Stockport

Wrap yourself in a blanket (on long-haul flights these are usually on the seat, on shorter hops ask the hostess). Cough and groan ostentatiously. When asked about your condition, explain that you are a medical mystery and have baffled doctors across continents, even now you are being flown to be seen by yet another specialist. Despite your repeated assurances that it is not contagious, you will find a cordon sanitaire around your seat. Thus, the rest of your flight will pass in comfort. I know that this works because a French woman I was supposed to be seated next to coming back from the West Indies one year did it. When I saw her practically skipping through the terminal building at Heathrow, I was so incensed by her deception I knew I had to have revenge. As we approached customs, I tipped them the wink that I suspected she was a drugs courier. Hearing the resonant snap of a rubber glove being pulled on gave me immense satisfaction.

Since I swapped my Nissan Micra for a big red BMW, people no longer let me out at junctions and abuse my rights on roundabouts. Why?
JH, Halesworth

Because nobody likes a show-off.

While sailing the Virgin Islands this summer, we partook of liquor one evening at a little place called Foxy's on Jost Van Dyke. Clearly, it was somewhere where patrons consume large quantities of alcohol, since pinned to the roof of the bar were, among other things, items of male and female underwear. I wanted to contribute but was unsure of the protocol. Is it the done thing to simply act on the spur of the moment and donate what one is wearing, or should one take along freshly laundered and pressed Y-fronts?
CL, Cheshire

I hope you are right about this. On some of these smaller islands, the bars double as general stores, in which case your sudden removal of your pants and offering them to the barman to hang up would be as appropriate as my whipping off my knickers in M&S and telling the girl behind the till to 'stick these with the others on the shelf over there'. I have no idea what the protocol is, as Mr Mills and I believe that underwear is best left at home when one is on holiday. After all, that is largely why one goes in the first place.

What is the best way to drive through a plate-glass window?
DGB, Aberdeenshire

When nobody's looking.

After someone has kindly let me into a long queue of traffic, what do I do if someone else then wants to join in front of me? If I let them in, will the kind person behind become irate because I am making them

even later, or will they think what a mean so-and-so I am if I don't?
WL, Wigton

There are no hard and fast rules here. Some days one should be extravagantly courteous, allowing other traffic in at every conceivable opportunity, stopping at all pedestrian crossings and red lights, and not opening one's door just because a cyclist happens to be riding past. On other days, however, one should nudge through the throngs of pedestrians refusing to give way on crossings, tailgate police cars as they cut a swathe through the jam with blaring siren, and sit rigidly staring ahead in the diamond box at a junction hopelessly blocking off traffic attempting to cross it. There is no particular reason for this; it is just what I have observed everybody else doing, and it certainly makes life more interesting.

Recently, I was sitting in the lounge of a hotel along with a dozen or so other residents, all quietly reading our morning papers. A young man came in, opened his bulging suitcase and proceeded to use his mobile phone for a number of calls. What do you say to a person whose bad manners are so blatant?
FHL, Ormskirk

Sigh, tut loudly and roll your eyes. If you are particularly peeved, you may also rustle your newspaper loudly when turning the page.

Last year, I booked into a hotel with my English boyfriend and arrived early afternoon. Owing to conjugal excitement, our bed was in considerable disarray when we went out later. On returning in the evening, the bed had been neatly remade. Thus the staff had to make the bed twice that day. Should we leave an extra tip in future? On another note, please warn your readers: I had a nice card at Christmas from the hotel and an offer of low-price rates at Easter. Had

we booked in my friend's name, the niceties of the hotel would have had disastrous consequences if seen by his wife.
SL, Italy

Your letter is a mite confusing because you mean 'adulterous' or 'deranged with lust' rather than 'conjugal'. Hotels can always spot guilty couples and treat them well knowing they are likely to become regular customers, but you should have left an extra tip to ensure their discretion. The hotel's sending of the card was a warning shot. You are at their mercy. They can ruin your life simply by confirming the presence of your lover at the hotel to a mystery caller from Britain or perhaps 'inadvertently' sending on an itemised bill to his home address listing champagne, flowers and the services of a chiropractor. Affairs are always risky, and there are more rewarding hobbies. Making lampshades, for example, would occupy your fingers much more profitably.

My problem is postcards. Every time I go on a visit, even if only for a day, I am compelled to send cards to all my friends, family and even myself. Apart from the cost, it takes up a lot of time writing them. I could stay at home, but that would be boring. Any other suggestions?
AT, 'Historic Ledbury'

Save time by writing them at home and posting them before you go.

MRS MILLS SAYS   Drink it first. Wash in it afterwards. It never works the other way around.

How to Deal with Everything Else

At the Table

THE TABLE IS A FRAUGHT PLACE, A BATTLEGROUND of ego and snobbery. People worry about how to behave, what to eat, how to fold napkins, whether to call it pudding, dessert or sweet, what cutlery to use and whether fish knives are really naff.

Many people who write to me even believe there is a whole elaborate edifice of eating skills and manners that needs to be mastered if one is to conquer 'society'. I know that they are thinking of such diktats as lettuce leaves should never be cut but folded with a fork; bread should be broken into small pieces, never bitten into; asparagus is only to be eaten with the left hand; pears should be peeled with a teaspoon . . . Regarded as hard and fast rules, this is all a lot of nonsense.

In fact, all table etiquette is elegantly simple and sensible at bottom. Cutlery is no great mystery: you just work inwards with each course. Each set is designed to make eating the particular dish before you easy, but actually it doesn't matter: if you decide to eat your lobster thermidor with a teaspoon, fine. People worry that making a mistake might mark them out as someone who has never eaten an artichoke or oeufs à la neige before. But what would be so terrible about that? Why are we all so anxious to be expert gourmands? Far more rewarding is to declare ignorance. The best meals I have had in France have been when I have told waiters I have never tried a particular dish or wine before. They always go out of their way to make sure I know how to enjoy it and get the best out of it.

Most seemingly arcane rituals turn out to be straightforward answers to otherwise complex problems. Passing the port in strict clockwise rotation around the table at large formal dinners, for example, ensures that everyone gets a turn. Imagine the chaos if the decanters zipped back and forth, hither and yon, to whoever cried the loudest, and someone would be bound to hog it.

The fish-knife snobbery is most bizarre. It came about because the fish knife wasn't invented until later in the nineteenth century, thus really smart people, who had inherited Georgian silver, did not have them. They used two forks to slide their Dover sole off the bone. Possession of fish knives therefore marked the owners out as jumped-up Johnnys-come-lately nouveaux-riches in trade. How could they live with the shame of it?

Once I was going into a very formal dining society feast in Cambridge alongside a young man whose white tie get-up included his wearing white cotton gloves. I congratulated him on his elegant attire but couldn't resist mischievously adding, 'One so rarely sees gloves nowadays. You know, of course, that a gentleman never removes them.' He nodded with alacrity. A flicker of alarm crossed his face when the first course turned out to be asparagus drenched in hot melted butter, but he soldiered on and ate the lot with his gloves on. They became soaked in oily butter, which congealed revoltingly, but he put up with the discomfort all evening. Months later, the dinner was written up in *Tatler,* which commented approvingly that members of this particular society were such sticklers that they even wore white gloves especially to eat asparagus. (This also tells you a lot about the kind of people who work on *Tatler.*)

Instead of worrying about what the rule for tackling a particular dish might be, consider instead what is the neatest way of dealing with it for the situation you are in. For example, if you are dining alone at home, it is easier to peel and eat an orange with your fingers. But if you are at a grand dinner wearing your best clothes and adorned with jewellery, you will find that the best way is to peel the orange with a knife and fork, because you don't want sticky fingers and juice dribbling everywhere.

Of course, to very many, much of this ritualised dining is now quaintly bizarre and as anthropologically diverting as the manners of the natives of Papua New Guinea. Canteens of cutlery (with or without fish knives) are hardly commonplace in a world where the dining table itself is fast becoming a rarity, and when people bother to eat at a table at all, it is in the kitchen rather than the dining room. The dinner party lingers on, however, as a competitive environment, a setting for show-offs and ingrates, as my correspondents have borne ample testament.

In the end, it is not just on special occasions that eating properly matters. All society's ills boil down to the fact that not enough of us sit down regularly at a table to eat. Though seemingly casual, gathering for a family meal is a good way of introducing some basic social rules to children, not only to do with the act of eating – keep your mouth closed, don't pile up your plate with more than you can eat, don't elbow the person next to you – but also to ritualised social interaction – listening to other people, giving others the opportunity to talk. On few other occasions do families gather without distraction. I do not count watching television together as a worthwhile experience in this way, and if there is one simple law that would change the world for the better, it would be outlawing eating in front of the television and making people sit down and eat together at a table.

And none of this cooking of several different dinners nonsense. You'll have what there is and if you don't like it, you'll go without . . .

When one eats After Eight chocolate mints, does one take the mint out of the wrapper and leave the empty wrapper in the box, or should one take the wrapper as well and discard it separately?
HN, Edgware

The rules are the same as for Ferrero Rocher chocolates: the wrapper should be rolled into a ball and flicked at the person opposite, preferably when they are least expecting it.

I have been to three dinners recently where the tickets made it clear that drinks were to be purchased separately. At the first dinner, a man down the table said 'pass the red', and that was the last seen of my wine. At a second, the man next to me helped himself to my mineral water and passed it round. Drinks were only sold before dinner, so I was unable to replace it. Finally, at another dinner, I ordered a half-bottle of wine. The man opposite helped himself and drained it. All these men were complete strangers, so I said nothing. What should I have done?
Mrs LP, Potters Bar

Do what I do: take a hip flask and keep it about your person between swigs – the cleavage is both convenient and discourages light-fingered men (at least in the early part of the evening). Alternatively, if, unlike me, you feel that 16-year-old single malt is not the perfect accompaniment for any meal, take a very large glass (or small bucket) so that you can empty any bottle you order as soon as it arrives.

Life is too short to drink bad wine, so if I am invited to dinner I always take along something decent. All too often, however, this is whisked away, never to be seen again, and I have to drink supermarket plonk all evening. Is there a discreet way I can persuade my hosts to uncork my offering?
JP, Newbury

'Open this now, or I'm going home' would probably work but may be deemed offensive by more sensitive souls. You could arrive with it already uncorked. Or, better still, drink it all before you get there, additionally ensuring that you don't have to share it with anyone else.

I am very proud of my table linen and to show it off I like to fold it in intricate ways – the bishop's hat being my favourite. A close friend has recently implied that this habit is naff. What do you think?
JLS, Rotherham

It's your house, you can be as naff as you like.

Do you have a position on the hostess trolley?
ADF, Maidstone

I have always found the wheels too unpredictable to make them reliable, as they have a tendency to skid away from Mr Mills and me at the most exciting moment.

I am a keen cook and enjoy giving dinner parties, which I plan meticulously. The timing of the cooking, as anyone who has set foot in a kitchen knows, is crucial, so nothing irritates me more than guests who are late. One couple we know regularly roll up an hour and a half after the time they were invited. What can I do? They are my husband's oldest friends, so he doesn't want to 'drop' them. Nor can I rely on their being exactly 90 minutes late and adjust the time accordingly, as sometimes they are only 30 or 45 minutes late. The rules of hospitality seem to forbid the rest of us starting without them.
Mrs KY, East Grinstead

There is a duty to be a good guest, just as there is to be a good host. These people overstep the mark. There is nothing wrong in starting without them: do it a couple of times and they'll get the message. However, nothing

is worse than the dinner party where everyone has begun to relax, conversation is flowing with the wine, mild flirtations are being conducted across the table and just as pudding arrives so do the latecomers, stone-cold sober and needing introductions. In a moment, the convivial ambience has collapsed like a soggy soufflé. My preferred tactic is to make sure the dining table is positioned by a window, the curtains are open and the doorbell disconnected. Start without the latecomers, and when they eventually turn up, ignore them. Don't even look round when they press their anxious faces against the window. The next day, express dismay that you failed to realise they were outside all the time. This is even more effective if you make them especially envious by having someone famous round for dinner: Robert De Niro, say, or Ant and Dec. In the event of their being unable to make it (clash with filming schedule or babysitter crisis), you can always hire a dummy from Madame Tussaud's: Liz Hurley is a good one and indistinguishable from the real thing.

I fear my wife has gone mad. She wants to hire a string quartet for our next dinner party. Isn't this unbearably pretentious?
PT, Bridgend

It all depends on the size of your house. If you live in a three-bedroom semi, I'd settle for a little mood music on the electric organ.

I am a fussy eater and can't bear, among other things, avocados, runner beans, celery, any kind of fish or peppers. I am also terribly shy and hate to cause a fuss. Is there any easy way to avoid these horribly common ingredients without upsetting my hosts?
TH, Norwich

Draw everyone's attention to something in the room. 'What a lovely electric organ,' for example. While they are all looking the other way, flick the offensive foodstuff onto your neighbour's plate.

When should one drink advocaat?
Mrs JL, Chester

Any time after your 75th birthday.

When dining out with my wife, she chides me severely for leaving my knife and fork crossed on the plate, lying in a four o'clock and five o'clock position. She favours the parallel six o'clock position. I am considering only taking her to the fish-and-chip shop in future.
CP, Durham

Your wife is quite right. Your cutlery habits are disgustingly slovenly. The parallel position is not only aesthetically pleasing, it also silently, but clearly, signals that you have finished the repast. Americans are notorious for flinging down their 'eating irons' (as they call them) any old how, although most of them only use a fork, anyway. This is partly because dining knives are so difficult to come by in the United States. The manufacturers, terrified after a series of legal actions brought against them by hapless Americans who contrived to stab themselves in the cheek while eating a 'hamburger with pecan pie sunny-side up to go' (as I believe their national dish is called), have withdrawn them in 47 states.

After this reply appeared in *The Sunday Times*, I was criticised in an American magazine. A Mr John Lehndorff called my remarks on their eating habits 'an ill-mannered attack on America'. Mr Gerald J Bodoh of Corvallis, Oregon, who sent the cutting, also enclosed a letter to correct me on several points: 'Nobody calls eating utensils "eating irons". Virtually nobody eats with a knife, except possibly Brits. There has been no "series of legal actions" by people who have stabbed themselves in the cheek. Manufacturers have not withdrawn knives from any state. There is no such dish in the US as "hamburger with pecan pie sunny-side up".' I am happy to set the record straight (although I thought Oregon was stuffed with cowboys chomping 'chow' with 'eating irons'). If other readers find their prejudices about Americans' lack of irony confirmed, don't blame me.

What is the best way to deal with the dinner-party guest who turns up roaring drunk?
WD, Portsmouth

These disruptive souls need to be removed quickly. I find that a pre-prandial game of blind man's bluff (blindfold the culprit and spin him round three times) followed by aromas of lobster thermidor, or any dish with aniseed and fennel, usually results in the sot staggering off to the bathroom and staying there. (This is only advisable if any noise made there cannot be heard at the dinner table and you have another for the more well-behaved guests to use.)

Why all the brouhaha about couscous when it is only semolina and steamed vegetables?
JRM-W, Agadir, Morocco

I wouldn't know, never having eaten brouhaha.

At a dinner party, I was horrified by a human hair in my quiche lorraine. I was trying to remove it discreetly when a fellow guest brought it to everyone's attention, causing me extreme embarrassment. What should I have done?
MO, London NW6

Quiche lorraine at a dinner party! How insulting. You should have calmly eaten the hair and pronounced it much more satisfying than the quiche.

We have a VIP, who is left-handed, coming to dinner at our home next Saturday. I am anxious to please and propose to set his dinner place the 'wrong way round'. My wife says this is arrant nonsense. What do you think?

AQ, Elsenham

Your wife is right. You would just be drawing attention to his disability, and, anyway, most left-handers eat the right way round. The less we do to mollycoddle these attention-seeking show-offs the better.

Predictably, I had several letters from left-handed readers complaining about my reply to AQ of Elsenham. Unfortunately, I was unable to decipher a single one.

At the end of a meal in our house, it is usual for each member to indulge in a yoghurt or similar delicacy such as a mousse. These occasions would be very enjoyable for all concerned were it not for my mother's dogged insistence on placing the dessert containers in a bowl or on a plate. This was useful many years ago when my brother and I would quite often spill our food, but I think that, at the ages of 16 and 14, we have now outgrown this stage. Please could you let me know if there is any specific reason for my mother's strange behaviour. She claims that it makes the dinner table appear more 'tasteful', but I do not see how this can be a valid argument as the containers often have huge yellow labels reading '25% off' on their sides, which is surely anything but tasteful.

EL, Leeds

While there is a debilitating condition of rampant preciousness (the kind that can't see a loo roll without hiding it in the skirts of a china doll), I do not think that is what is wrong with your mother. Of course, she is pretending that this is what is wrong with her, but only to hide from you her real problem: guilt. Her family are gathered around the table expectantly and what is put before them? Homemade spotted dick with thick, creamy custard? Apple crumble sprinkled with cinnamon? Warming rice pudding? No, a small plastic container of mass-produced, chemically enhanced

processed filth that has cost her no effort at all. No wonder she is driven to trying to rescue some self-esteem by going through the empty ritual of insisting on serving it in a bowl.

I recently discovered that as the port is making its rounds at a formal dinner, I need not worry if I 'miss the boat'. It is acceptable to send my glass around after it, to chase the bottle as it were. However, when I was in a situation to try this out, I found that I did not have a clue how to initiate such an action and ended up waiting as usual. Any suggestions?
TTT, Cambridge

This seems very odd to me, as it means everyone sitting between you and the bottle will be interrupted. Perhaps a better solution would be to lean forward and yell at whoever has the port, 'Oi, baldy,' (or some other suitable distinguishing-feature-based epithet, assuming you don't know his name) and then to slide your glass along the table to him cowboy-saloon style. However, at this stage of the evening, one usually finds the octogenarians are staggering off to relieve themselves every ten minutes. You should take advantage of this by rushing into any empty seats as the port approaches, thus you can knock back several glassfuls and be ready in your own seat by the time the decanter returns.

I am curious to learn if it is considered de trop to offer one's host's dog a slurp from one's soup bowl by carefully placing it on the floor by one's chair, or should one lift the animal onto one's lap in order for it to drink at the table? I am asked out less often these days but would still like to know.
HL, Hove

It depends on the size of the dog. (Mind you, if anyone tried to pull a stunt like that in my house I'd drag them outside and tie them to the drainpipe with a length of hairy twine, unless it were a particularly hot day, in which case I would lock them in the back of the car for a couple of hours.)

I am an out gay man determined to maintain standards of protocol. I do admire your ability to modernise issues of etiquette. When I have a dinner party with mixed gay and heterosexual couples, should I seat people boy/girl or hetero/gay?
WFM, London SE2

Gosh, modern living is complicated, isn't it? I always find myself wondering, what does one do with the bis? After several absolutely disastrous evenings, I have come to the conclusion that it is best to stick with the boy/girl arrangement, regardless of gender.

If you are round at someone's house for dinner, is it rude to ask for another gin and tonic?
GHJ, Clapham

Yes, you'll never be invited back. The trick is to draw your host's attention to your empty glass subtly. For example, I find that leaning right back while draining the last droplets of melted ice then toppling into a heap on the floor never fails to draw attention to my alcohol-deficient predicament.

Having made the acquaintance of a rather splendid widow, I want to take the next step in social intercourse by inviting her back for a romantic dinner for two. To impress, should I provide a sweet, a dessert or a humble pudding for afters?
LH-S, Sudbury

Yawn, yawn, yawn. It's nearly the next millennium, so let's not waste time on the class divides of English vocabulary. If she's satisfied with your spotted dick, she won't care what you call it.

Why is it that people's manners are now so bad? I like chums' company, so ask people for dinner fairly frequently, but so rarely do they ever ring me to say 'thank you'. I live alone and need friends and like giving hospitality, but I would so like to be thanked and, indeed, asked back.

AG, Wilts

After your next dinner party, buy yourself a case of champagne. Write to each of your guests thanking them for this generous present, explaining that the postman had left the package on your doorstep and their attached note must have gone astray. You assumed it was from them as you had received thank-you notes from all of the other guests. Say that a simple card will be satisfactory in future.

We have a dear friend who, as he lives overseas, we only see occasionally. His hospitality exceeds all possible expectation. However, we dread the meal ending, as we know that we will be asked to watch some three or four hours of holiday videos. How can we avoid this ordeal without hurting the feelings of our friend?

PC, Camberley

Having suffered from this appalling behaviour myself, I can only repeat what I learnt then: never enter a strange living room without slipping a hairgrip into the slot of any idle video player, just as a precaution.

My husband and I have been invited to a silver-wedding dinner by neighbours who attend my dinner parties. They are a delightful couple: she's very plain, he's loud, and I think they live on their pension. They said they wanted the party to be different, and, my God, it is. It's in a fish-and-chip 'restaurant'. What does one wear for such an occasion? My husband says it will be fun, but I'm not sure. I have never been to a fish-and-chip restaurant before. Would you and Mr Mills accept such an invitation? I think perhaps we should go away to the country for that weekend.

DT-S, Hove

You have to go for their sakes. Stiff upper lip and all that, but just because you are good sports and prepared to enter into the spirit of the thing doesn't mean you have to go the whole hog – heavens, no. Otherwise people might think you did this kind of thing all the time. So take along your own cutlery and china and insist that the staff use it for you and your husband. At several points, exclaim very loudly, for the benefit of the whole restaurant and not just your table, 'Isn't this fun? We've never done anything like it before, but if this is slumming it, count us in for the next time, darlings.' I believe that the recognised dress for someone like you on this occasion would be a fur coat and no knickers.

A number of years ago, most food packages were marked 'untouched by human hand', and this gave a certain reassurance. Now, in the numerous television cookery programmes, food is mixed by cooks with bare, be-ringed hands who have an occasional nose pick. What are we to think?
JWHD, Herts

Things have got better. 'Untouched by human hand' meant it was all done by machines injecting chemically enhanced slurry into tins and plastic boxes.

MRS MILLS SAYS

Leaning right back while draining the last droplets then toppling into a heap never fails to draw the host's attention to my alcohol-deficient state.

Health and Grooming

CONTEMPORARY MORALISTS WOULD HAVE US believe that we are the most vain generation ever to mince across the earth. We are obsessed with our bodies, pushing ourselves for perfect muscle definition in packed gyms, skipping to plastic surgeons for lifts, nips and tucks, shooting botox into sagging brows and zealously following rigidly prescribed diets. This might be true in LA but not really for the rest of us, with the possible exception of parts of Cheshire.

This is not to say that vanity isn't rampant. Of course it is, but then it always has been, just as there has always been a lucrative trade in cosmetics and body treatment from the ancient Egyptians onwards. Most of us avoid anything too drastic and soldier on with a bit of slap and a new hair-do every so often.

Americans, particularly New Yorkers, are always staggered by the paucity of nail salons and how expensive it is to have a manicure in the UK. What they don't realise is that there is still a great deal of subtle snobbery in Britain towards excessive body maintenance. Having one's nails done regularly is regarded as a bit 'common'. You can't muck the stables out and maintain a decent French polish. And you can usually place a woman's social position quite precisely by the state of her lipstick: smeared on haphazardly in one quick swipe with barely a glance in a compact? Upper. Strongly defined lip-liner outlining plump, pouting, glistening mouth? Almost certainly a glamour model from Chigwell.

Plastic surgery used to be completely beyond the pale, only resorted to by desperate pop stars, fading actresses and members of the working class with nothing better to do. It pains me to say, however, that as the surgeons have become more skilled and the results no longer look quite so grotesque, so we have seen cosmetic enhancement being embraced by formerly more sensible parts of society. To my amazement, I even know someone who has had a 'procedure', although she swears she'll never be seen again in a bikini. I think that's a blessing, as it is not seemly for a woman of her age, and crepey cleavage is never a good look anyway. At the moment, as I am perfectly happy with my own appearance, I think this kind of surgical intervention is dreadful, but I expect I might change my mind in a few years' time.

Judging by my postbag, the main bodily concerns in Britain today are body hair, halitosis and flatulence. A swift glance and sniff around the office or bus will confirm that this is quite right.

I don't like my bottom. What should I do?
CMcM, Ireland

This is very subjective. Just because you don't like it doesn't mean everyone else shares your opinion. Bear in mind you have the worst view of it, too – all that twisting round to look at it in the mirror. Seek other opinions and have it photographed so that you can assess it properly. I have no doubt that you will be surprised at its many fans.

I have decided to follow in the footsteps of many celebrities and drink my own urine to improve my health. Although I am now firmly placed among the

middle classes, I come from a humble working-class background and find this to be a disadvantage sometimes. Does one drink urine from a glass, and is it served chilled or at room temperature? My father drank only Bass beer, nothing else would do, so I was not taught the niceties that surround other beverages.
Mrs CG, Stafford

Drinking urine is one of the giveaway signs that someone is middle-class. No working-class person would be so stupidly modish. It is correctly drunk from a Mongolian hand-carved loving cup while squatting on a pre-seventeenth-century Ibo birthing stool, or from a Murano wine glass while lying back on a Le Corbusier recliner (all available at the Conran Shop). I don't believe it makes any difference to your health, apart from having a radical effect on halitosis.

In view of the fact that your personal view on hair, expressed recently in your column, is that men should shave only their faces and women only their legs, should I dare suggest to my wife, who happens to be called Juanita, that she remove those hairs from around her nipples that give the impression that two spiders have landed on her breasts?
JGC, Seville

Why bother? I imagine they keep the flies down in the bedroom.

I have fabulously long nails that my boyfriend enjoys feeling run down his back. The problem is that face creams, hand creams and so on always collect underneath the nails and take ages to clean out. Do you have any tips?
Miss SL, Sussex

The whole point of long nails is that they are time consuming and high maintenance, thus signifying that you are a lady of leisure. So don't complain, or

people will start to think your nails have ideas above your station. This being Britain, there is a strong body of opinion that believes long painted nails are 'common' and 'tarty', and a sure sign of working-class origins. Although I have quite long nails myself, this is purely to indulge a peccadillo of Mr Mills. We find that giving free rein to relatively harmless fantasies in the privacy of the home, with the doors firmly locked, helps sustain a healthy marriage (as well as being good aerobic exercise).

I would like to know if there is an effective way of getting rid of the swimming-pool hog. Usually male, aged between 40 and 65, overweight and balding, he strides aggressively to the 'no diving' notice and dives in. He then proceeds at a very fast pace down the middle of the pool, with arms and legs thrashing wildly. The ensuing tempest results in the pool emptying of other swimmers very quickly. The hog generally carries on for at least half an hour, and only the most intrepid of swimmers dare go into the water. What can the ordinary swimmer do about this problem?
LP, Herts

Complain to the management. 'Good grief,' I hear you cry, 'I can't imagine that being very effective.' But it will be if your complaint is that he urinates in the pool as he swims. The embarrassing scene that will follow will discourage him from ever returning to that pool, even if he manages to convince the attendant of his innocence.

I have an embarrassing problem. I'm quite a large person and suffer miserably from BO. My entire social life has plummeted dramatically. I have no friends at present and am forced to stay inside due to my incurable misfortune. The only friendliness I receive now is the odd Christmas present, which nine times out of ten is a bottle of deodorant. These hints are not welcomed, and, believe me, I've tried everything but without success. Matters have become so bad that I

have had to start working from home. Please help, as I am in desperate need of advice.
IS, Harrogate

Working from home is very sensible. You are doing all the right things. A social life is completely overrated. If you do feel cut off from normal human intercourse, I believe there are young ladies that people like you can phone and talk to for a very modest fee, young ladies so selfless that they make themselves available to chat 24 hours a day, and if that isn't a kindness in this day and age, I'd like to know what is.

A colleague frequently passes wind during conversations. He appears not to notice. This really puts me off my train of thought. How can I subtly mention this to him, as I think he is unaware of what is happening?
RH, Preston

This phenomenon can be technically called 'social schizophrenia'. Ostensibly, he is very well mannered, but his body is rebelling against the bourgeois constraints of his social self. To put it more simply, you are obviously either talking utter nonsense or saying something he profoundly disagrees with, but he is too polite to say so. His body, controlled by his unconscious, however, is busily farting at you. So, it's your problem, I would say.

In the past few weeks, while travelling by bus, I have noticed that nobody wants to sit next to me, preferring instead to stand. (Usually my husband drives me, but he has recently been away on business.) My free bus pass is due, and I was excited by the prospect of journeying around Essex, but now I feel as if I could be subjecting myself to endless deprivation. Whatever shall I do?
GG, Rainham

Try washing.

I suffer from appalling bad breath. I have tried mouthwashes, mints and breath fresheners; I have tried cleaning my teeth after every meal; I have even tried changing my diet. Nothing works. People still visibly flinch when I open my mouth. What can I do?
MDM, London

Learn to breathe through your ears.

Apart from holding one's breath, what can one do about a smelly armpit hovering above one's nose while being served in a restaurant?
CJ, Malaga, Spain

Learn to breathe through your ears.

Why is it that celebrities, minor royals and supposedly well-educated people attend clinics and pay vast amounts of money to subject themselves to the unnecessary, unbeneficial and potentially dangerous procedure of colonic irrigation? Is it because it is undignified, uncomfortable, expensive and brings tears to your eyes, so it must be doing some good?
NCA, Bradford

The bodily functions exist to remind us that all men are created equal. However, if you can pay someone else to perform your bodily functions for you, you must be one up on the rest of humanity.

How do you know if you are wearing too much aftershave?
JR, Brixton

When strangers start talking to you in French. An English person will say, '*Quel dommage, monsieur, vous n'avez pas de savon en France,*' while Johnny Frenchman will say: '*Ah, bonjour mon compatriot. Voulez-vous prendre un verre de vin avec moi?*' (Probably.)

Because of some bowel trouble, I have the unfortunate habit of breaking wind in company. What is the proper thing to do in this situation? Smile and treat it as a joke? Ignore it and pretend nothing has happened? Look suspiciously at someone else? Apologise profusely?
WG, Carlisle

Stare suspiciously at the shyest person, as they are unlikely to protest and will probably blush, too. If there is a dog present, kick it. Make sure, however, your own body language does not betray you. A slight tensing of the facial muscles and widening of the eyes, combined with the raising of a single buttock, followed by a sigh of relief are a giveaway, I have often found. If you have the misfortune to make a noise, laugh immediately. This alleviates everyone else's social anxieties, and they will all collapse with laughter, too. Farting, as only we British with our sophisticated sense of humour understand, is just very funny.

Apart from raising them from time to time, what else can I do with my eyebrows?
TS, Radmer, Austria

What an innocent you are. Unfortunately, as this is a family newspaper, I cannot explain further, beyond saying you obviously have no idea of the delights you are missing.

I am an accomplished pianist as well as a competitive athlete. My friends tell me that I am also very good looking. Which part of my body should I insure?
KB, Aldershot

If you are as arrogantly immodest in life as your letter manages to be, I would insure your teeth. Some lesser mortal is bound to take a swing at you in a fit of envious pique.

Why is it that men with a lot of body hair go bald at an early age?
BAL, London

Simply to emphasise the boundless unfairness of life: not only do they feel hideously self-conscious about their shiny domes generally, they also feel awkward about going to the swimming pool and frightening small children who think some kind of weird monkey is on the loose (and can be encouraged to shout the fact quite easily, I find).

Following hospital treatment for haemorrhoids, the consultant explained how to spot a fellow sufferer by the way they sit. Can you suggest an opening conversational line so that I might befriend a fellow sufferer?
WT, Herts

'Better out than in.'

What is your opinion on the increasingly vexed question of armpit shaving?
PL, Kettering

No lady should shave any part of her body that stands more than 18 inches off the ground. Conversely, no man should shave any area of his body below the neck. There is no good reason for this, other than that I find the sight of goosepimpled five o'clock shadow under a woman's arm revolting, and men who shave their chests just make my skin crawl.

I am keen to get fit and to start going to a gym in the new year, but I am worried about exposing my puny body in front of all the fit, sleekly muscled people who will be there. How am I ever going to build myself up if I cannot overcome this initial hurdle?
JMJ, Birmingham

Wear an overcoat until you feel sufficiently well endowed in the pectoral area.

I am cursed with insomnia. Every night I toss, fret and turn while my husband snores obliviously away by my side. I have counted sheep, drunk hot milk, had hot baths and read the whole of Proust. Sleeping pills worked, but I don't want to keep on taking them. Any suggestions?
Mrs MEJ, Norwich

I know what you are going through, as it happened to me. The solution turned out to be simple: I lie very still in bed, pretending I'm asleep, and, before I know it, I am asleep. Of course, you need to have an incentive to maintain this pretence, and, for me, nothing works as well as Mr Mills feeling amorous. So if I feel insomnia looming, I whisper suggestively to Mr M as he drifts off to sleep; a few moments later he is wide awake and raring to go while I cling to the edge of the bed imitating the deep respiration of slumber. Despite the tutting, sighing and muttering from my now restless husband, I find I soon drop off. Marvellous.

It's so unfair that my adolescence is plagued by acne. Is there any medication or useful tip you might know of to rid me of this perfidious plague?
WW, Dorset

There are various advanced treatments for acne now available from a doctor, but he or she has to be pretty worried about you to prescribe them. On the whole, I believe, the medical profession is content to regard acne as a useful way of keeping the teenage pregnancy rate down (fat chance). You'll grow out of it, but in the meantime look out for a spotty girlfriend.

My boyfriend and I disagree on toothpaste. He likes Colgate Whitening while I prefer Mint Fresh. How can we resolve this dispute?
ML, Sheffield

Blessed as I am with the wisdom of Solomon, the solution came to me in a flash: buy two tubes of toothpaste.

I have become very self-conscious about my hairy upper lip. I have thick black hair and, increasingly as I get older, a moustache to match. I worry that if I shave I will stimulate its growth and may be left with five o'clock shadow. Is bleaching the answer?
Ms DL, Cheshunt

All the remedies are fiddly. Live with it, but change your name to Juanita.

A shower-happy friend of mine says people who have baths lack hygiene because they have to put their dirty feet in first. Is he right?
NV, Taunton

Not entirely. Apart from the feet, there is the sweat and grime that coagulates in all the other interesting nooks, crannies and deep ravines of the body. Just imagine you are wallowing in that fetid ooze every time you lie in a bath. So, yes, showers are more hygienic, invigorating and Scandinavian, but baths are so much more sensual, more replete with erotic possibility and far easier to read *Woman's Weekly* in.

An advert on television says the best toilet paper is soft tissue. What evidence do they have? Out of seven people I asked to comment, five said hard, one said soft and the other threatened to call the police. Advertisers seem to think the public are daft.
DRM, London

It is disturbing to think there are people out there who prefer hard, shiny toilet paper. Get real: it's like trying to mop up with cellophane and as comfortable as dragging sandpaper across your eyeballs.

I consider the invention of soft toilet tissue a useless abomination (re letter from DRM of London). I refuse to use it. Luckily, I can still obtain 'hard' medicated paper, though at a ridiculous price. (Sample enclosed.)
PM, Harpenden

Examining the enclosed sample, I think you have been using coarse-grade sandpaper. But if you're happy, who am I to interfere?

Please enlighten me as to the social etiquette involved on encountering one's GP or bank manager naked in the shower at the sports club.
GJG, Wimborne

Doctors are easily dealt with as they adore talking about ailments and you have the ideal opportunity to bring up those little niggles that are ordinarily (and so unfairly) deemed off limits. What could be simpler than offering him (or her!) the chance to examine your piles or fascinating itchy patch? Bank managers should be studiously ignored, but make sure you get out of the shower before them and hide their clothes. I know this is a petty, mean-minded gesture, but so is failing to honour a standing-order payment because it would put your account £3.26 in the red for two days before your pay cheque goes in. After he has spent 20 minutes begging, make sure you charge him a £20 'administration fee' for telling him where his clothes are.

Dear Ms FR, rest assured, although I may have laughed, a doctor certainly won't, so there is no need to be embarrassed. I gather they are used to removing far stranger objects.

Dear Ms FR, I am delighted that it has come out of its own accord and, no, I haven't told a soul.

MRS MILLS SAYS

Seek other opinions about your bottom and have it photographed. I have no doubt you will be surprised at its many fans.

Dress

EITHER MOST PEOPLE KNOW HOW TO DRESS OR hardly anyone goes to events that require observing an elaborate dress code, for I very rarely receive letters inquiring, for example, whether miniature awards may ever be worn with black tie, or diamonds before the cocktail hour.

There's no stuffiness these days; you can wear what you like. At least that's what we would like to believe, but it isn't entirely true. While rigid rules for formal wear have relaxed considerably, dress codes are more complicated and subtle than ever. My husband recently had to attend a residential conference. The programme included advice on dress for the various events and dinners: it ranged from 'Smart Casual' via 'Relaxed Casual' to 'Casual (Party)'. Mr Mills wore a suit.

We are adept at reading the signals. The combination of deck shoes, canvas jeans, polo shirt and moleskin jacket (some quite possibly in very loud colours) equals middle-aged middle-class man at the weekend; Camper shoes, combat trousers, long-sleeved T-shirt, hoodie (but hood importantly not up) under leather jacket equals middle-aged creative (or would-be creative) type on a Wednesday. And at a time when clothes have become so cheap, it is not so much what you wear as who made it. The label, often now the most important part of any garment, has moved to the outside.

Clothing is very tribal. If you live on a council estate, it is apparently necessary to advertise the fact by wearing nylon sportswear, just as wearing a dark suit of heavy woollen cloth is de rigueur on even the hottest day if you work in the City.

Dressing for many women is a consuming passion: indeed, many seem to regard it as the reason they were put on the earth. Men may declare themselves content with two pairs of shoes, black and brown; women need not just a whole rainbow of colours but also combinations of colours and varying heel heights. Oh, and boots. Slavishly chasing after fashion always makes women ridiculous but ignoring it completely will make you look like a fusty eccentric, unless you have tremendous style and confidence. I tend to favour a consistently formal style of dress: tailored skirts and jackets. It is more flattering on the figure as one moves away from youth, and absolutely nothing looks worse than women of a certain age packing themselves into the garb of the young. Middle-aged midriff spilling out from under a crop top and hanging crepe-like over hipster jeans has been one of the most unpleasant sights of recent years.

Most letters I have received on the subject are from people seeking enlightenment about the baffling fashions sported by others outside of their own tribe – because they belong to a different generation or social group. Many of the others are purely practical.

Often these days, one comes across the phrase 'smart casual' on party invitations. What does it mean?
JL, Romford

Wearing the most expensive clothes you possess. Formal clothes tend to follow basic designs that make it possible to get away with cheaper imitations. With

men's suits, for example, only the practised eye can tell apart the £400 off-the-peg number from the £1,800 bespoke job. Casual clothes, however, are about labels and designer faradiddles that apparently make one white T-shirt £60 better than another. Sadly, we all seem to be acutely aware of all of this. Personally, I make it a rule never to go to a party described as 'smart casual'.

Should one use only cufflinks with a chain-link connection or are those with a solid bar, the end of which swivels, now socially acceptable?
BM, Liverpool

The chain-link is Victorian; the solid-bar swivel type of cufflink is a 1950s innovation. The latter is easier to insert into a cuff and less likely to break, but naturally people of taste would not dream of sporting anything so unspeakably nouveau.

My wife refuses to wear stockings as she thinks they are tarty.
RL, Leicester

She is absolutely right, but that is the point of them.

Occasionally I wear a bow tie. I tie this by having the longer end in my left hand. Recently, I purchased one with a pattern of parrots and daisies. When I tied it, the pattern was upside down. It was only by tying the bow with the longer end in my right hand that I achieved the correct pattern. This I find rather difficult to do. Has the bow tie been badly made or have I been tying it wrongly?
BM, Liverpool

Burn this offensive item of clothing immediately. For any man below the age of 57, bow ties are only acceptable in plain black or white (with appropriate accompanying dress), with the obvious exceptions of professional clowns and affected barristers.

When buying shoes, I invariably walk out with the wrong size. I recently bought a lovely pair of sandals that fitted like a dream in the shop but three hours later had produced painful blisters. When I was a child, the Clarks measuring machine always took the size decision for me. What do I do now that I'm a grown-up?
RG, Chelsea

Small children are not very good at determining whether a shoe fits or not. As we get older, we can try on a shoe and tell whether it is comfortable. What's more, from one week to the next we can remember our shoe size. Do you expect your hairdresser to give you a lollipop for sitting still? To find a plastic toy in your muesli? Shoe retailers rather rely on their adult customers to be grown-ups.

Why should men be expected to buy a shirt without first trying it on? Collar size alone will not tell them whether they will be able to button it, wet their cuffs while washing their hands or even look decent without their trousers on. Women, on the other hand, try on as many blouses as they like before making a choice. Where is all this sex equality?
JC, Gibraltar

What a strange man you are. Why do you want to get your cuffs wet? And, surely, the whole point of removing trousers is to look indecent? Anyway, your dilemma is easily solved: switch to wearing women's blouses. You'll be able to try on as many as you like and strike a blow for sexual equality at the same time.

Most fashions these days seem to be designed for lettuce-eating human rakes – and certainly not for those who, like me, have watermelon-like buttocks. Do you have any bottom-hiding tips?
GC, London

Apart from avoiding high-cut swimsuits, there is little you can do. Everyone knows that voluminously flowing

robes simply shout 'fatty' (ever seen Kate Moss in a kaftan?). Otherwise, edge around rooms with your back to the wall and sit down a lot, making sure you choose wide armchairs. My uncle George laughed so much he swallowed his teeth when the vicar's wife wedged herself in his Parker Knoll.

I dread having a visible panty line when I wear tight-fitting jeans or trousers, but I just cannot bring myself to wear a thong or G-string. What should I do? It is tempting – if rather draughty – to abandon underwear altogether. But I'm afraid of seeming like an old slapper. Please advise.
CI, Newcastle

Try bloomers, those marvellous pants that have legs elasticated just above the knee and a waist that fits snugly under the bust.

Some friends and I have come across a worrying dilemma, namely, which drawer should underwear be kept in? Most of us believe that it should be the top drawer, but there are some dissenters who think the bottom drawer is correct. Who is right?
Miss HW, Llandegfan

Strictly speaking, the bottom drawer is a special place for keeping all those things that mean a lot to you, that you treasure but rarely wear, or that you would rather forget about: old love letters, silk evening gloves and cardigans that your granny knitted. I blithely assumed everyone kept underwear in the top drawer but was staggered to discover this was not the case. When I asked my friend Samantha where she kept hers, she replied, 'Anywhere my husband can't find it.'

Are cufflinks better than buttons?
IJ, Fulham

Not on shirt fronts.

All my shoes have started squeaking. I am a solicitor and dignity is all, so if I have to walk across my office when clients are there, I feel compromised by my shrieking footwear. What is going on and what is the solution?
GFC, London N1

The reason old shoes develop squeaks is due to sweat. The only solution is to start wearing flip-flops.

The elastic in my Y-fronts has slackened so much that the only way to keep them up is to fold and staple the waistband to reduce it. Should I buy a smaller size so that when the elastic fails, they still fit?
MF, East Sussex

Simply wear them with a pair of braces.

I want to buy a new dinner suit and rather fancy one with a white jacket. However, I am anxious not to commit a faux pas. What is the correct etiquette for wearing a white jacket?
GS, Tonbridge

Men of a certain age reach a point where they fondly imagine a white dinner jacket will instantly make them as debonair, sophisticatedly cosmopolitan and suave as James Bond. Forget it. Unless you are the spitting image of the young Sean Connery, they have all the sophistication of a chocolate-brown brushed-nylon dinner suit.

My wife is reluctant to repair the little loops in the back of my coat collars, which are invariably broken. She contents herself with facetious remarks about my forgetting to remove myself from my coats before hanging them up. Should not coat makers think less about the width of lapels and the number of useless buttons on the cuffs and concentrate instead on beefing up those vital loops?
TH, Coventry

The snapping of coat loops is distressingly frequent, and I have my own solution: simply sew a coat hanger into the back of all your overcoats. Not only is broken-loop misery banished for ever but your coats will keep their shape better, too.

Rubber, leather or Lycra – what would you recommend?
MB, Kirkcaldy

Call me old fashioned, but cotton every time. The absorbency makes it so much more comfortable.

Recent years have been very good to me. I have prospered enough to realise my ambition of joining the local hunt. Yet, even after having been a member for a year and being extremely generous whenever contributions and donations were required, my pleasure has been constantly marred by the lack of manners and unfriendliness of the other members. The matter came to a head at a recent meet when a sudden downpour threatened to spoil the pleasure of my immaculately groomed fellows. Although I handed out large (and quite expensive) umbrellas, the members showed absolutely no gratitude, and I was astounded by one lady, who said, 'No, thank you, I would rather get drenched than be a moving advertisement for your f***ing mobile-phone company.' Do I simply have to get used to the fact that these people lack the breeding that they would like us to believe they have, or do I need to change my approach and offer some other form of gift? If you advise the latter, could you suggest something (preferably tax deductible with a unit price of about £30)?
DJP, Kent

I suspect they just feel a bit awkward about accepting gifts, but they will soon come round if you carry on, especially if you present them with things they really want. For instance, hunting coats are pricey and get old and tatty quickly, so why not have some run up with your company logo across the back in canary yellow? Of course, you will win some members over more quickly than others, but as soon as the rest see how smart your coats look in the field, they'll be beating a path to your door.

I dislike ironing. I became a widower early in life and brought up four children. I did all the ironing. Heaven knows how the subject came up, but over a drink at the bowling club with six others, it was clear that they only ironed the collars of their shirts if necessary. Underpants, vests, boxers, pyjamas, never. And four of these men had wives. I iron everything except socks, as otherwise I would not feel totally dressed. Should I stop ironing? Your opinion is important to me, as you have shown good sense in previous replies.
FF, Laoghaire

Yes, of course you should carry on ironing. Just because the rest of the world is descending into slovenly habits there is no need for all of us to follow suit. Being properly turned out is not merely a matter of appearance, it is also a moral position, inextricably linked to your sense of self-worth. What value does a person who dresses like a tramp put on himself? It may be fashionable for today's pop stars to look like a dog's dinner, but will their careers last as long as Cliff's? (He's always smartly turned out, with beautifully pressed slacks. He must be a martyr to his iron, that man.)

What is the optimum length for shorts (assuming underpants are worn)?
M&JA, Liverpool

The length of shorts is determined by dividing the length of the leg by the width of the thigh. The lower that number (i.e. the thicker the thigh) the shorter the shorts may be. However, they should never be shorter than half the waist measurement. The beauty of this time-honoured formula (which I just invented) is that it prevents fatties from prancing about in obscenely

DRESS

short shorts, while ensuring that skinny weaklings wear shorts that cover their weedy knees. Underpants should be worn at all times with shorts, as the possibilities for embarrassing disasters are too distressing to consider.

What is the correct way to wear a top hat at a wedding: behind the ears (thus causing them to stick out at an alarming angle) or covering?
JG, London W9

Your hat is too big. It should sit above your ears, unless they are abnormally large, in which case all hats are best avoided, with the sole exception of balaclavas.

How I pity you suffering women with wire-cupped bras, elasticated girdles, buttock-revealing bathing costumes digging deep into the crotch and cramped toes wedged into pointed shoes. Is all this torture worthwhile simply to create an image of beauty?
ES, Algeciras

From the overheated tone of your letter, I'd say the answer was yes.

Can you please sort out a disagreement my friends and I have been having: if a boyfriend buys you expensive jewellery or clothes, is it tasteless to wear them once you have split up? If not, does it make a difference whether the item in question is worn in front of the ex, or behind his back, and what is acceptable once a new lover comes along?
AZ, Romford

It all depends how vindictive you want to be. If some chap has given you a £30,000 pearl necklace and then had his head turned by some little trollop, I should flaunt the pearls in front of him at every available opportunity. But if some bloke has given you a gold-plated chain with his name emblazoned on it as a token of 'true love for ever', I would give it back to

9

Darren forthwith. As for wearing items in front of new lovers, if it's simply a nice blouse, there would be no harm, but if it's a pair of fur-lined crotchless panties, I'd let them stay in the drawer.

I love my large collection of knitted ties, but my wife says they make me look like an old fart. Who is right?
DM, London N10

It depends what you wear them with. She'd be right if you disport yourself in baggy cardigans and Crimplene slacks, but simply combine one with a taut leather G-string and whimsical expression and you'll really put the wind up her.

The label on my underpants recommends washing at 50°C on a cotton cycle. I am confused because it does not offer guidance as to how long I should wear them before washing, nor in what fashion they ought to be worn. My normal practice is to wear them for three weeks and then to wash them, whether they need it or not.
DM, West Yorkshire

At the moment you don't seem to have a problem, so let's leave it for a few months, then you can write to me again. ('Dear Mrs Mills, despite my sunny outgoing personality, I don't seem to have any mates, girls won't talk to me and people move away from me in crowded places . . .')

We are an ordinary middle-class family with two teenage children, a boy and a girl. My vegan brother, aged 43, is getting married for the first time in May. The wedding is to be a 'pagan' wedding, held in a teepee in north Wales. What should we wear?
Mrs SL, Enfield

Wellies.

What are we to make of the new trend for rings worn not only on the index finger but, as in my daughter's case, on the thumb? Once upon a time, according to Mme de la Tour, the index finger signified willingness to marry, the second engagement, the third marriage, and the little finger no wish to marry. What on earth is my daughter telling me?
Mrs R De M, Cornwall

'I am a free spirit, a rebel, an outlaw on the fringes of respectable society. You cannot confine me in your smug bourgeois world of boring middle-class values and materialistic pig-grubbing. Oh, and can Dad pick me and Harriet up when the concert ends, about 11.30?'

When I wear my wife's tights, the hairs on my legs stick out through the material. I have persuaded her to buy opaque pairs, but this seems to add to the problem, as the hairs catch the light and show up even more. I am at a complete loss as to what to do. Any suggestions?
ET, via e-mail

Wear trousers under your tights.

It is very common at meetings these days to take off one's jacket and very common to see braces. I have always worn a belt, having been brought up to think it was vulgar to show your braces. What is the etiquette in this matter?
PKV, Edinburgh

It is preferable to be seen wearing braces than wearing trousers around your ankles, unless your underpants are particularly exciting.

I have noticed that there is a certain kind of woman that frequents rural pubs on Sunday lunchtimes and insists on wearing her shirt or jacket collar erect. Why do they do this?
RH, Leicester

This look is usually combined with a string or two of pearls and, in fact, is the accidental result of their forgetting to turn their collars down after slipping the pearls on. It would be appreciated by all if you were to point this out to them.

I am a 16-year-old girl who has an urge to pierce my navel, despite parental opposition. They threaten it will become infected, but I still want to do it. The trouble is my parents are my doctors, and, if it does get infected, I would have to show them. They'd only say, 'Told you so.' What should I do?
IEM, Cheshire

Call me old fashioned, boringly sensible or the voice of sanity (depending on your age/desperation to be trendy), but I cannot understand the urge to make holes in one's body. We do not live in a rainforest where, I am sure, there is a good reason for pierced flesh and distended lips. We do not expect our young men to strut about wearing penis sheaths fashioned out of gourds. My grandmother always advised against following fads and fashions on the grounds that looking like everybody else was 'common'. Wise words that kept me in homemade clothing until quite late in life when I finally realised what everybody was laughing at. So I am with your parents on this, as not only is there a danger of infection but also of complete deflation. You don't want to look like last week's party balloon, do you?

How can I stop my wife throwing my most comfortable and treasured clothes in the dustbin? She just does not understand that men's clothes take years before the newness wears off. She says she is not comfortable with the effect my clothes have on our 'image'. I say fashion is for people who have no style. She tells me not to stand in the street on bin day. What can I do to make her see sense?
RR, Blackpool

Ralph Lauren once told me that when an American becomes rich he buys a new sweater; when an Englishman becomes rich he inherits one. Old clothes can be stylish, but they have to be the right kind of clothes in the first place: a shirt with a frayed collar must be Jermyn Street, not Mr Byrite; beaten-up shoes should be Church's brogues, at the least, not something from Clarks in grey. Anything with a whiff of synthetic fibre about it should be consigned to the dustbin as soon as it looks the slightest bit tired.

Would you wear a bright yellow shirt when going out?
PL, Bedford

Yes, but not with that tie.

Here in Solihull, a surprising number of younger women have given up wearing knickers on most occasions. One commented to me that her skirts were long enough for modesty, and she enjoyed the feeling of freedom. Their private choices are, of course, not my business, but the open way some of them talk about it makes me feel uncomfortable. Am I being unduly prudish? If you made that choice, would you tell your female acquaintances?
Mrs JR, West Midlands

I have never mentioned it to anybody.

Last week, in quest of a pretty dress, I entered a little boutique in London's Beauchamp Place. An assistant looked me up and down, and asked what I wanted. 'A pretty dress for a wedding, size 16.' 'Well, madam, as you can see this is only a small shop, so we do no sizes over 12.' I was perplexed: after all, a dress on a hanger takes up the same space in a showroom, no matter what size it is. Do you think I should only shop in large stores from now on?
AG, London WC2

The more expensive the dress, the smaller it will be, but that doesn't necessarily mean it won't fit you. The shop assistant was not saying that you were too big, but that you looked too poor to afford their clothes.

MRS MILLS SAYS

Men of a certain age fondly imagine a white dinner jacket will make them as sophisticatedly cosmopolitan as James Bond. Forget it.

Miscellaneous

IT IS VERY GRATIFYING THAT READERS FEEL THEY can write to me on any matter that is bothering them. Thus I find myself with a large collection of uncategorisable one-offs on such matters as missing bedroom doors, ownership of classic cars, dealing with the Inland Revenue, wrestling with Velcro and methods of unwrapping sweets quietly at a concert.

Social historians in the future will probably ponder the issues raised in this section in the belief that light will be shone on the most vital concerns of our age. They will be wasting their time.

Last week, I was reading *The Tale of Mrs Tiggy-winkle* to my daughter when I was struck by the reference to a 'pocket handkerchief'. Surely this is an oxymoron. What other type of handkerchief could there possibly be?
Mrs WM, Northampton

Like much of Miss Potter's work, it is now out of date. Handkerchiefs used to come in all manner of sizes. Think of cigarette lighters. Table lighters used to be as common as smaller ones for the pocket, so it was with handkerchiefs. The table handkerchief was just that: a large piece of cloth for communal use. Of course, the practice died out in the eighteenth century and

people began referring to it simply as a 'tablecloth'. Strictly speaking, you would be quite right to blow your nose on the tablecloth the next time you are at a dinner party, but I gather the practice is somewhat frowned upon nowadays.

I recently found out that one of my close friends unremorsefully performed sexual acts with my now ex-boyfriend behind my back. I am a calm person by nature, but in this exceptional case, would it be acceptable to hit someone smaller than me who wears glasses?
NRG, by e-mail

Generally speaking, it is not acceptable to hit small people who wear glasses, but I find it is much safer.

My mother-in-law was recently approached in a bar by a young man who claimed to be a representative for a modelling agency specialising in 'the more mature lady'. Mum was truly smitten by the chap and is convinced she has a great belated career ahead of her as a 65-year-old supermodel: she talks constantly of 'late-flowering beauty' and is becoming quite intolerable. This is all very well, but, on further investigation, it transpires that the agency is merely a facade for recruiting women of a vulnerable age to the pages of a magazine specialising in 'blue-rinse babes'. How can we put her in the picture without breaking her heart?
JY, Ryde, Isle of Wight

At 65, your mother-in-law hangs around in bars being picked up by young men. I would not worry about her at all.

I suffer terribly from irritating tune fixation – the tendency to get a particularly maddening melody stuck in my head, sometimes for days on end. Having spent the best part of this morning under the influence of 'Silver

Lady' by David Soul, I am now spending the afternoon trying to fend off Haircut 100's 'Love Plus One'. Is there an easy mental exercise I can perform to purge me of such irritations for ever?
WH, London WC1

A tune running around one's head is the brain in neutral, the engine idling. The quality of the music is entirely dependent on the quality of your taste, so you have only yourself to blame for suffering from such low-grade tosh. There is no known cure, although developing an exclusive taste for Schoenbergian serialism should curb such irritating outbreaks – unless you are pretentious enough to attempt humming the whole of *Verklärte Nacht*.

I keep on encountering people I thought were dead. It can be quite a shock. One lady I bumped into last week, whom I thought had died years ago, asked me if I was all right, adding, 'You look as if you have seen a ghost, dear.' The trouble was, I thought I had. How can I stop this happening to me? And what should I say to the people in question if it does?
AJO, Trinity, Jersey

How do you know they are not dead? Jersey's a strange place that would keep *The X Files* going for years. 'You're looking well considering . . .' would probably be your safest reply.

I was shocked to see on the television the rows of men wearing Elvis masks at the recent Edgbaston test match. Who are these idiots who watch cricket wearing ridiculous masks and wigs?
Mrs JF, London

I think you'll find that they are eminently respectable bankers, insurance brokers and accountants, whose offices believe that they are ill at home.

I was enjoying reading your column in the garden yesterday morning when I went indoors to make a coffee. Returning five minutes later I was flummoxed to find the lawn covered in straw. Have you any suggestions as to how it got there?
DK, Ross-on-Wye

The most likely explanation is that it was blasted there by the downdraught of an alien spaceship landing in a nearby field. So be on the lookout for crop circles in your area. A more far-fetched explanation is that during the summer, hot air forms small twisters that pick up bits of detritus, such as straw from a recently harvested field, and carry them considerable distances. In America, of course, we are led to believe these are much bigger and pick up houses, but I don't believe they really exist outside of the perfervid imagination of Hollywood.

Slapping suncream all over oneself to avoid burning is all very well, but what do you do if the smell makes you queasy?
JL, Ipswich

Always wear a suit.

How can I prevent the assistants in shops from calling me 'mate' and the security staff from shadowing me?
BO, London NW8

Always wear a suit.

A colleague at work is inordinately proud of his old Fiat. How can I let him know that everyone laughs at his car behind his back, one that not even hairdressers would drive? I accepted a lift from him once and cringed with embarrassment as pedestrians openly pointed and laughed. He regarded it as affectionate acknowledgment of his car's classic status.
TN, London W11

Why spoil everyone's fun? Besides, there is no hope for him. Once a man becomes attached to a car, he drops out of the human race. His sense of humour vanishes as his sense of proportion is blown to pieces. It probably costs him far more to keep roadworthy than any run-of-the-mill recent car. It is all too telling that a friend's husband told me recently that at a certain clinic, among the top-shelf magazines supplied to help men concentrate on the job in hand, was a copy of *Practical Motorist*.

I am sure you have noticed how noisy sweet wrappers are. I was wondering if there is any possible solution to opening them quietly, as they make so much noise that it is embarrassing for people, especially during dreary sermons or chemistry lessons.
Miss M, Bristol

Suck them with the wrappers on. Not only is this quieter, it's kinder on the teeth. And the sweets last longer, too.

Why do I fail to win competitions – especially crosswords – despite submitting the correct solution? Also, why did I fail to receive any prize while holding premium bonds from 1958 until 1996? Having cashed in the bonds and invested in the national lottery, why is it that I have never won even the smallest of prizes? It goes without saying that any letter I write to a newspaper remains unpublished. Am I unlucky or just insignificant?
JH, South Croydon

Nobody in Croydon is allowed to win anything. Similarly, I think you will find that if you monitor the letters columns of all newspapers for the next year this will be the only time that the words 'South Croydon' appear, so make the most of it.

Why is it that whenever I have just bought something, friends immediately announce they have a spare one in the attic I could have had, or their brother-in-law

could have got one for me cheaper? Should one take these offers seriously or avoid mentioning such things to friends in case not using their services spoils the friendship? I usually pretend I can't remember the price or that it was given to me as a present.
PW, Colchester

This happens everywhere, but especially in Essex. The correct response is to say, with a tone of regret, 'Oh dear, if only I had known.' Never take up one of these offers, you will always be disappointed. If you mention in the pub that you are thinking about spending £3,500 on a computer, someone will splutter into his beer and say, 'You what? I know a bloke could get you one for £500, tops.' Take him up on his offer and you will end up parting with £800 for a 1980s word processor made in Bulgaria with a Cyrillic keyboard and obsolete floppy disks. It is mistakenly thought this is a peculiarly male phenomenon, a testosterone-fuelled sport of one-upmanship. Not so. A friend of mine wanted a hat for a wedding. She envisaged something wide-brimmed and dressed in ostrich feathers, a kind of Cecil Beaton creation for Audrey Hepburn. 'Oh, I've got one,' a mutual acquaintance said. 'You can borrow it.'

'Has it got a brim?'
'Yes.'
'Feathers?'
'Of course.'

Unfortunately, the hat could not be produced until the morning of the wedding. Thus my friend found herself wearing a green trilby with a tatty budgie's wing on one side and looking for all the world like Brunnhilde in mufti.

The other day I bumped into a neighbour sloping out of Sainsbury's looking decidedly edgy. He was carrying a multipack of toilet rolls. When I asked if he was a 'new man' doing the weekly shop, he told me in an embarrassed whisper that he had done the shopping yesterday, but his wife had insisted he return to exchange the toilet rolls as they were 'the wrong

colour'. Have I witnessed the final emasculation of the English male?
MPB, Market Harborough

The English male was emasculated long ago. But I am still aghast. Everyone knows that white is the only permissible colour for lavatory paper.

Imagine my horror when, having been invited to stay with friends, I discovered that they had removed all the bedroom doors and put curtains in their place to create more space.
KG, Crawley

Next time you are invited to stay, take a spare door with you. It is easily accommodated on a car roof rack and makes a wonderful table in the event of an impromptu street party.

On the TV quiz show *University Challenge*, why is it obligatory to take a sip of water after answering a question correctly?
RS, Heathfield

To avoid looking smug. (Perhaps Jeremy Paxman might benefit from following their example.)

What is the recognised fail-by date for new year resolutions?
MT, Shrewsbury

Three o'clock yesterday afternoon.

How can I cure myself of having to acquire an item (any item) from the hotels that I visit?
Ms P, Portsmouth
PS Please find enclosed a very useful pencil.

Before you leave your room to check out, ring down to reception and, disguising your voice, say, 'The woman in room X has got a suitcase stuffed with tacky toiletries

and a scratchy bathrobe.' With a bit of luck, you will be stopped and asked to open your bags in the busy reception area. Imagine your embarrassment and humiliation. You need only do this to yourself a few times before you finally start to get the message.

I have observed for some time that the women of my household, who number three, have the peculiar habit of squeezing the toothpaste tube near the top, or at best halfway down, while I, and others of the male sex, take the more logical approach and squeeze from the bottom up. Does this, in your opinion, prove conclusively that the male is the more efficient and logical?
SP, Treorci, Rhondda

No (because toothpaste habits are unreliable indicators of wider epistemology).

All my best friends have died this year. How do I start again?
Mrs AG, Wilts

Well, to start with I'd keep quiet about the fatal effect being acquainted with you can have.

I live on a rural estate near the sea. You couldn't imagine a more peaceful and quiet setting. However, the tranquillity is shattered at dawn by the dreadful hooting of wood pigeons. I've tried earplugs, but to no avail. Not wishing to shoot the noisy tuneless irritants, I turn to you in desperation.
DGM, Newport

Fine, I'll pop down and shoot them for you.

I have long been a staunch supporter of Friends of the Earth and have always been willing to contribute generously to their funds, yet they still haven't sent anyone to dig my garden. Could you advise me

as to whether I should refer this matter to Trading Standards?
GC, Warwick

This is typical of charities today. Environmentalists rush halfway across the world to 'save' some unsightly chunk of rainforest, but when it comes to a bit of weeding in their own back yard (so to speak), they get all hoity-toity. Pruning roses is beneath them, planting out a few cuttings and hoeing a couple of beds is not good enough. Yet just because you haven't got a flock of orang-utans swinging through your lime trees doesn't mean your garden is any less important to the environment. Sadly, this argument won't get them turning up on your doorstep with a broken fork and a ball of hairy twine. You need to take more drastic action: threaten to redevelop your lawn as Heathrow's fifth terminal. They will be round like a shot, digging holes all over the place, erecting new fencing, making interesting 'features' in the trees (sleeping platforms, very useful if you do plan to introduce orang-utans) and climbing Nelson's Column to unveil a banner (not horticulturally necessary but still pretty impressive). Your only problem then will be getting rid of them.

I have always wondered how concert-goers standing shoulder to shoulder in packed stadiums manage to answer the call of nature. Do you have any idea?
EG, Aberdeen

I have my suspicions. It wouldn't surprise me one bit if they waited until the interval and then availed themselves of the facilities lurking behind those ominous doors marked LADIES and GENTS. Mind you, I have come to have my doubts about that fountain stuck in the middle of the Prommers. It'll be a long time before you catch me drinking from it again.

Whenever I am alone in the house, I have the most outrageous fantasies. Should I worry?
MJD, London N3

As long as you stay clear of anything that involves props, you'll be fine.

As an Australian living abroad, I often mingle with expatriate English, some of whom appear to have elevated their social level. I am often put down, as Australians are considered by the latter to be descended from convicts. I would be grateful if you could equip me with a few cutting remarks to be used in self-defence.
ELS, France

The expatriate English have something to hide. It is why they live abroad. They are not all criminals, of course, but all will tremble if you can hint that you know anything of their past. Reginald 'properties across north London' is usually Reg the owner of two lock-up garages in Dalston; Clifford 'the movie biz' is Cliff the pornographer with two linked video recorders and a bulk purchase of Bulgarian tapes. If you want to get on with these people (and heaven knows why you would), you have to appeal to their snobbery. 'My great-great-great-great-grandmother was Captain Cook's mistress' and any connection with the royal family will have them eating out of your hand. I'd try 'Princess Margaret smoked my didgeridoo' or 'Prince Charles lost my boomerang', if not both.

I would like to be a novelist. I would be so good at talking about my oeuvre, and I am quite attractive, so would photograph well. I have a brilliant Booker Prize speech worked out, and a *South Bank Show* special on me and my work would be fascinating. I have all the right connections, and my father is very influential. The only problem, or fly in the ointment as we writers might say, is that I find it impossible actually to sit down and write for any length of time. Can you give me any advice?
Miss SL, London

While being feted by intellectuals at smart launch parties and hobnobbing with the likes of Salman Rushdie, Melvyn Bragg, Tom O'Connor and Bruce Forsyth is an

attractive prospect, writing a novel is immensely boring. It is best not to write it yourself but to get someone else to do it for you. The world is full of writers desperate to have their work published, but they fail because they don't have the right connections, whereas you certainly do. Find a disgruntled scribbler and offer to get his work published. He might baulk at the thought of it going out under your name, but point out that his chances of getting it published otherwise are virtually nonexistent. (Please send my regards to your father.)

Every time I try to watch football on the television, I fall asleep after about five minutes. Should I seek medical advice or simply consider myself fortunate?
FJF, York

No, this seems a perfectly healthy reaction, though avoid watching Arsenal, as you might slip into a coma.

The increasing use of spiral staircases in areas used by the public raises an important question of etiquette about which the relevant literature is universally silent. Should I allow a lady to pass on the inside, shorter route where the stairs are narrow and more difficult to negotiate, or on the outside where the stairs are wider and safer but the journey longer? My careful observations over a ten-minute period in a bookstore show clearly that there is no natural rule emerging. We urgently need a definitive statement. Can you please help?
Dr DGH, London N6

My own experience of men and spiral staircases would suggest that it depends whether you want to try and look up her skirt or not.

Should I remove the variety/country of origin stickers from individual apples, pears, etc., before serving them to dinner guests, or would this breach EU regulations on

food labelling? I find the information imparted by the stickers has a very stimulating effect on conversation around the table, but there is always the danger of a guest inadvertently choking.
ML, Witney

They are not just fiddly little labels, they are bureaucratic fascism invading our lives. I didn't fight in two world wars (obviously) just so that my fruit could be disfigured. Do they think we are all stupid? I don't decant a pound of coxes into the fruit bowl and five minutes later discover I've forgotten what they are. We must fight back. Every time you go into the supermarket swap the labels around: transform Jamaican bananas into South African granny smiths, turn Lebanese passion fruit into Israeli oranges. Fruit is only the beginning, by the end of the decade we'll all be required to be personally labelled on the left cheek: country of origin, best-before date and bar code.

My local Tesco, being in a university town, is frequented by a number of our European cousins. They insist on talking loudly in strange tongues, usually across aisles. We British take our shopping seriously, as it is, of course, our new religion. The supermarket is our new cathedral. What can be done to make it known to our foreign visitors that British shopping, like our sex, is a quiet activity?
PW, Colchester

Sex 'a quiet activity'! Certainly not in our house. I think it is you, Mr PW, who is out of step with the rest of us. There's nothing like a bit of full-throated yodelling to make things go with a bang, I find. No, the only time that sex should be quiet and restrained is in the supermarket. However, to get back to your substantive point about Johnny Foreigner: it wouldn't surprise me if they use their own shops for shopping only and are thus shocked at the wealth and variety of extraneous activities that take place in a British supermarket, viz., slapping small children, heavy petting in toiletries and the purchase of particularly nasty nylon socks.

I recently moved to Brighton from the Midlands, and relatives and friends assume I will welcome them with open arms during the summer. I moved for some peace and quiet, not constant visitors looking for free bed and breakfast. I have managed to put them off for this year by saying I will be busy decorating, but how do I refuse them in future?
GL, Brighton

Announce that your house is now a B&B and although you would simply love to have them to stay, it is not cost-effective. It's easy to run a guesthouse: stock up on nylon sheets (orange and green), make sure none of your curtains draw over the whole window and put up a sign saying 'No children or dogs'. Advertise your rates as £150 a night (including continental breakfast, bathroom on every landing and TV lounge) and you won't be worried by guests either.

When I was told my parents would be invited to my friend's wedding reception, I naturally passed the news on to them. Last week, my mother was very hurt when an invitation arrived for me but not them. My instincts tell me this is an oversight rather than a deliberate snub. Should I approach the bride's parents, send a fake invitation to my parents or smuggle them in as the cabaret?
PG, Bingley

Your instincts are wrong. I can guess at once what has happened, and it's purely financial. The bride's parents counted up the guest list, multiplied it by the cost per head of the reception and immediately cut back on numbers. By all means have a word, but you won't get anywhere unless you suggest that your parents bring sandwiches (and a flask of tea to toast the happy couple). Smuggling them in as the cabaret would only work if your mother can sing 'Una Paloma Blanca' while your father plays 'The Birdie Song' on an accordion.

Having been a keen whistler all my life, I now have a tendency to whistle medleys of popular tunes of my youth while engaged in domestic chores. My wife finds this harmless habit irritating. When a child, she was informed that well-behaved little girls did not whistle. I have realised that very few females whistle. Is this due to cultural factors, or does whistling have a biological function as a mating call?
AP, Burscough

It is entirely due to cultural factors. 'Well-behaved' is in fact a euphemism for 'people like us': put bluntly, whistling is lower-class behaviour only indulged in by tradesmen and other riffraff. Women, being naturally more socially attuned, understand this better than men.

Several old buffers I know use the titles 'colonel' and 'squadron leader'. Does this mean the armed services are employing septuagenarians, or is it a rank they once held? Is there a minimum rank that you can use? My father was a private during the war, does that mean we must now refer to him as Private W? Or is it, as I suspect, merely an affectation with no rules or regulations?
JW, Oldham

Ex-servicemen are entitled to use the rank they attained. Lower ranks usually don't bother. To be known as lieutenant in your fifties is merely to draw attention to the fact that you were a bit of a duffer. Generally speaking, your title improves with age. If you leave the army in your thirties as a captain, you are entitled to the rank of major by your fifties and colonel in your seventies.

When our favourite costume dramas on television come to an end, we love to watch the titles. However, we are at a loss to know what exact role is played by a gaffer, a best boy and a grip. Please enlighten us.
Mrs AC, Lewes

The few proper jobs in film making are pointing the camera in the right direction, switching the microphone on, shouting 'action', finding the money to pay for it all and acting. These people are known as the camera operator, sound recordist, director, producer and trouble. However, most young people now want to be 'in films', and so they hang around sets, doing odd jobs and wearing the right gear (climbing boots, padded waistcoats, baseball caps with official film logo, etc.). Because directors don't want to put 'sandwich carrier', 'drug supplier', 'satisfier of petulant actress's whims' and so on at the end of their films, they have invented a series of bizarre job titles, such as best boy, grip, clapper loader, assistant to the location focus puller, writer and so on. (The film rights to this column are still available.)

Why does my cat eagerly wolf down any meaty morsels donated from my dinner plate, yet has to be in the terminal stages of starvation before grudgingly nibbling at leading cat-food brands?
JP, Preston

The entire Darwinian point of cats is to make their owners' lives a misery – scratching the best armchair, moulting on duvet covers, refusing to be stroked by a loving child while rubbing against the legs of a confirmed cat-phobic, complicating holiday arrangements. I do not understand why anybody bothers with the wretched animals and would happily run them down were Mr Mills less squeamish (as it is, the philosopher FH Bradley remains one of my heroes, less for his thinking than for his hobby of creeping across Oxford at night shooting cats with an air rifle). If you really want your animal to eat cat food, simply pile Whiskas onto your plate and tuck in; the perverse creature will demand to share it with you.

What would you do if Mr Mills took a bite of food followed by a drink of water and made 'cement' while chewing? This habit drives me to distraction, but my husband says no etiquette book condemns his

behaviour. He is right: they do not mention it. We will abide by your decision.
Mrs TMC, Fulham

Etiquette books are silent on a lot of things – breaking wind in crowded lifts, sniffing underpants before putting them on again in a changing room, creeping up behind elderly relatives and shouting 'Heart attack!' – but this does not necessarily mean they condone these actions.

I am having trouble with the Inland Revenue. I am afraid that they will come and inspect my accounts to try and extract more tax from me. If they do visit, and I understand these visits are completely unannounced, how should I treat them?
BCM, Wolverhampton

Express surprise when they turn up, but invite them in and present yourself as an open, trusting soul, the kind of person who keeps his cash in biscuit tins around the house (have an example to show them). A good phrase to use with tax inspectors is, 'I'm sure we can sort this out without too much difficulty,' while proffering £40 in used fivers.

Why doesn't the Queen carry any money? Is it in case she tries to escape?
DB, Wallingford

The Queen doesn't carry money because she never needs to buy anything. She does not suddenly think, 'I could murder a Big Mac,' when she is halfway round M&S of a Saturday afternoon, probably because she eats sensibly and doesn't come over all hungry unexpectedly. If she fancies seeing a film, they close off Leicester Square and make all the actors turn up to see her afterwards, so this is probably organised a couple of days in advance, giving her the opportunity to put it on her credit card. Most theatres have a royal box she can slip into when she fancies seeing a show, *Phantom*

or *Mamma Mia!*, for instance. There aren't any what you might call 'local shops' near Buckingham Palace, so I imagine she has to send a servant off if she fancies a Mars Bar or getting a video out for the night.

I am 42 years old. Is there any chance that I might still have 'street cred'? How would I know if I did?
REC, Somerset

Street cred only applies to teenagers, and who in their right mind wants to be admired by adolescents with their wretched enthusiasms and dreadful earnestness? ('How dare you say it's just a phase. I shall always be a committed communist,' I remember screaming at my aunt when I was a 15 year old.) But all that is irrelevant for you anyway, as it is impossible for anyone from Somerset to have street cred in the first place.

Every night when my wife and I retire to bed, we each have a Werther's Original in place of a good-night kiss, as I imagine all people of pensionable age do. May I, through your excellent column, warn others of the dangers of swallowing one whole in bed?
MJP, Newtownabbey

Hey, kids, and you thought there was nothing to look forward to in old age. Then again, perhaps 'sucking a Werther's Original' is OAP slang for some perverse practice. If any pensioners want to spill the beans, drop me a line (but please, please, no photographs).

You wondered what Mr MJP meant when he wrote that he and his wife had reached an age when they had a Werther's Original when they retired for the night. Well, although not possessing any aphrodisiac qualities, Werther's Originals are a well-known sex aid for the elderly. Old-age pensioners suck them while making love. It helps them to remember how long it takes and when it has finished. (This is variable, of course, depending upon whether you have left your teeth

in.) For a sharper experience, with an encouraging efflorescence at the end, try a sherbet lemon. My next-door neighbour always has a Fisherman's Friend, but he's a bit odd. Werther's are overall the most reliable. An 8 oz pack lasts my wife and me a year.
BS (aged 68), Sheffield

After a night on the tiles with my best friend, she gave me an astonishing piece of advice. She said that due to the fact I am a single, childless, 41-year-old woman, I should refrain from revealing the truth to any man who chats me up lest he considers me 'desperate' and 'up for it'. I am confused now, as I have never felt my unmarried state should cause me any such problems. (I am relatively attractive and successful.)
C, Staffs

The fact that you are attractive and successful is the giveaway: your friend is envious and trying to curb your style. What's wrong with being 'up for it'? I myself am up for all kinds of things – WRVS committees, the parish council, the tennis club social board. Ignore her peevishness.

Is this writing paper rather vulgar? (It was a gift.)
Mrs SHB, Buxton

Yes, so I refuse to even look at the rest of your letter on principle.

I collected all the *Sunday Times* Brainpower supplements. I particularly thought issue three on memory improvement would be of great help to me, so I put it aside for further reading. Unhappily, I have forgotten where I put it and now cannot find it. Have you any suggestions?
SB, Lampeter

Look under the sofa.

What is the best way to deal with the problem posed by single friends bringing their new partners for the weekend? Is it better to make up two bedrooms and not ask the question or make up the one and make the assumption? Alternatively, does one ask the question well in advance of the invitation?
N and JW, Solihull

You can avoid the issue by making up two rooms and ignoring footsteps in the night, but what's the point of incurring extra laundry just through embarrassment at asking a direct question? I am happy for guests to do anything they like, as long as it doesn't damage the wallpaper or fuse the lights. (One word of advice: decline all offers to join in anything that takes place after 2 a.m.)

I sleep alone on an even bed. In the morning, I find myself dangling over the edge. Why do I do it and how can I stop it?
DER, East Sussex

You are moving around in your sleep because you are dreaming that you are a small seal having baby oil rubbed into your skin by a large Nordic-looking man with a blond beard who may be naked. You keep twisting to see (hence wriggling across the bed) but can't be quite sure, and anyway you are now a mermaid feeling the tingling cold sea water rushing over your naked breasts as you dive deeper and deeper pursued by a shark who talks like Terry-Thomas and has the same moustache. You disappear into an overgrown cave only to be caught up in the arms of . . . but now you're awake, dangling over the edge of the bed. That's exactly your dream, isn't it? I know because it happens to me. It is quite easily prevented, but why bother?

After two years, my satellite dish is looking grubby. Is there any company I can contact, or could I clean it in the dishwasher?
NE, Newcastle

The filth is a direct reflection of the kind of programmes you have been watching. Switch to wholesome nature documentaries and watch your dish recover its pristine sparkle.

How am I to deal with boring, unsolicited telephone salespersons offering me double glazing, fitted kitchens, etc? Do I dispose of them rapidly – my current record is a satisfactory seven seconds – or do I indulge them with tales of how imaginary aunts, who had such work done 'only last week', were ripped off or delighted, depending on my mood, and 45 minutes later tell them 'Well, not today, thanks.'
JG, Barnham

You seem to have the matter under control, but for variation you might like to try my method. I always say, 'Thank you but I don't have a phone,' and replace the receiver. This obviously engenders such bafflement that no person has ever rung back to argue otherwise.

I was born under the sign of Cancer, but I want to change to Taurus as they seem to have a much more exciting time. Is it too late to do anything about it?
AB, Alton

We are in the twenty-first century, for goodness' sake! Nobody has to live under a star sign they don't like. The Labour government is abolishing the House of Lords because of the iniquity of the hereditary principle. Similarly, people should not be denied the opportunity to become Capricorns because an accident of birth meant they emerged into the world at the wrong time of year. How preposterous and old fashioned that would be. I change my star sign every month, depending on which forecast I most fancy.

Do you find Velcro fastenings as infuriating as I do? If you're in a busy, crowded street, they stick to any passing furry fabric, causing sudden encounters

with strangers in crowds. Even when you are on your own, they stick to furry parts of the same garment, enveloping you with the ferocity of a straitjacket. Bring back the button, I say.
Mrs HB, Cheadle

Ever since it was invented, along with Teflon, Velcro has been one of the blessings of modern life. We have come a long way since its original use (fixing the lunar module onto Saturn V or some such), and I don't know where we would be without it. Tiresome small children can be slipped into specially designed jackets and attached to the kitchen ceiling (I know where they are, and they seem to enjoy it). Surgical supports can be more flexibly adjusted, and, as most of the nation has long since realised, Velcro has meant saying goodbye to sliding-antimacassar misery.

My father-in-law has an infuriating habit of not finishing his . . . I'm usually at a loss as to what to do when in conversation with him. Do I complete his . . . thus wrongly giving the impression that I think he's retarded? Or do I let the conversation flow, even though I usually haven't a clue what he's . . .?
EC, Whitley Bay

It is easy to cure someone of this habit: simply finish their sentences in an inappropriate manner. For instance, should your father-in-law say, 'Are you . . .?' and fade into silence, you should say, '. . . interested in your wife sexually? No, I think she's a bit old for me.'

MRS MILLS SAYS
The only time that sex should be quiet and restrained is in the supermarket.